23 STEPS TO SUCCESS
& ACHIEVEMENT

This book is dynamite. It will blow sky-high pessimism,
boredom, frustration and despair.

This book is a compass. It will guide you into new worlds of
interesting and happy living.

This book is a key. It will open the door to the realization of
your fondest dreams and the development of your hidden,
wonderful potential.

This book will work miracles. It will open your eyes
to more beauty, improve your health, release you from fear,
renew your confidence, give you new courage
and hope.

23 Steps to Success & Achievement

The Dynamic Plan that Will Change Your Life

ROBERT LUMSDEN

Thorsons

An Imprint of HarperCollins*Publishers*

Thorsons
An Imprint of HarperCollins*Publishers*
77–85 Fulham Palace Road,
Hammersmith, London W6 8JB

The website address is: www.thorsonselement.com

Published by Thorsons 1972
This revised edition 1999

1 3 5 7 9 10 8 6 4 2

A catalogue record of this book
is available from the British Library

ISBN-13   978-0-7225-3610-0
ISBN-10   0-7225-3610-0

Printed and bound in Great Britain by
Clays Ltd, St Ives plc

Contents

Step   *Page*

1. Better Health Ahead — 1
2. New Words for the Taking — 5
3. Increased Powers of Concentration — 9
4. A Much Improved Memory — 11
5. New Positive Emotions — 15
6. An Attractive Voice and Clear Speech — 18
7. More Tact Tomorrow — 24
8. Giving Your Boss a Better Deal — 28
9. Towards Improved Ideals — 32
10. Make Maturity Your Goal — 35
11. Happier Relationships Ahead — 40
12. Better Communications — 43
13. Getting More from Your Reading — 48
14. Problems are for Solving — 52
15. Increased Happiness for You — 55
16. Wider Mental Horizons — 59
17. No More Woolly Thinking — 63
18. A More Imaginative You — 67
19. Project After Project — 70
20. Going the Extra Mile — 74
21. Being a Better Parent — 78
22. All Serene — 82
23. Enrich Your Life Now — 86

Better Health Ahead

The First Step

You are probably already fundamentally healthy. Occasionally you may go down with a minor ailment, but basically your body is sound. If that is so, congratulate yourself. How about minor ailments? The first step in reducing these is to cultivate an attitude which revels in the happy thought – *I have no serious physical defect: my body is fundamentally sound*.

If your health has been poor, and one organ after another has been giving you trouble, take this thought to heart. Repeat it to yourself as you go to work. Say it to yourself whenever you relax. Let it be your last thought at night and the first as you wake. It's worth repeating, isn't it? *I have no serious physical defect: my body is fundamentally sound*.

Once you are convinced of this fact, your health will improve immediately. You will begin to trust your body more. You will expect it to function smoothly, to overcome disease, to resist viruses. Confidence pays good dividends here as in everything. It ousts fear. Soon a benevolent circle emerges – confidence improving health and improved health breeding confidence. You will usher in for yourself a new era of constant good health.

Treat Your Body Wisely

Many ailments are brought on by foolishness There are people who literally maltreat their bodies. Some years ago a naval rating decided to 'celebrate' his birthday by drinking the rum ration of *all* his messmates. In the drunken torpor which followed, he turned in his hammock and suffocated himself in his pillow. The consequences of too much alcohol are not always so tragic, but they are generally undesirable. If you treat your body unwisely you can't complain when it reacts unfavourably.

That fresh air is essential to life is a fact known by all. Yet many spend a lot of money and hours each day deliberately contaminating the air they breathe. The moral is obvious and reinforced by medical pronouncements on the relationship between lung cancer and smoking.

Some live to eat rather than eating to live. They stuff down large quantities of cell-clogging, fat-making food completely ignoring the findings of nutritionists. People in no sense gluttons are convinced they should never rise from a meal unless they feel 'full up'. This ill-becomes human beings; animals stuff themselves until they can take no more.

The general rule should be – *give the body what it needs in the quantities it needs*. Aim at a moderate, well-balanced diet. This will include adequate proteins, fruit, vegetables and water.

Take sufficient exercise – if your work doesn't provide it – with respect to your age. If you are over forty, take life more leisurely. Take time – as the poet puts it – to *stand and stare like sheep and cows*. Keep a watchful eye for the myriad beauties of life. In this car-ridden age, beware of never walking anywhere. Walking remains the best form of mild exercise.

See you get sufficient sleep. Most people require seven or eight hours, though some do with less, especially as they get older. If you don't sleep well, much in this book will help you. Meanwhile don't worry about it. It's not little sleep which harms you, but worry. Sleep comes easiest unsought. Cultivate indifference to it. Say to yourself: 'It doesn't matter if I *don't* go to sleep. I'm resting, I'm comfortable and I'm enjoying this delicious quietness.'

You Are Psychosomatic

This means your mind and body are interrelated. The term comes from two Greek words meaning 'soul' (or 'mind') and 'body'. Medical science asserts that the mind exerts an incredible influence on the body. A striking example is that of the *ghost* pregnancy, when a woman may so desire a child as to produce in her body all the symptoms of pregnancy and yet not actually have conceived. When X-ray photographs convince her she is not an expectant mother, her body returns to normal.

The positive thoughts and attitudes advocated at the beginning of this chapter will now be seen to be justified. Desire good health, think good health and expect it, and you go a long way towards ensuring it. Good health is your birthright. You *ought* to have it. Anything less is an imposition. From this moment, then, accept that your health is taking a turn for the better. *You are going to get healthier and healthier*. Radiant, abounding health will be yours.

Other Important Factors

Keep yourself happy. How to do this will be emphasized later in this book, but essentials are: (1) Come to terms with your job and learn to like it. Alternatively find one you *do* like. (2) Have at least one hobby – something which satisfies you. (3) Find time to serve your community, apart from your daily work. (4) Arrive at a philosophy of life, religious or otherwise. If it is atheistic you must accept its corollaries with courage and cheerfulness. On no account yield to bitterness or despair.

These factors will occupy and satisfy your mind, and with harmony there, your nervous system will be free from tension. This will result in your body functioning like a well-lubricated machine.

For the Handicapped

It has been assumed that the reader has all his organs, limbs and faculties. Suppose you are living with a disability? Much of what has been said will still apply. There's no reason why you shouldn't enjoy better general health.

Further, as you imbibe the principles stressed in this book, you will more easily rise above your difficulties. New interests will enter your life. A new attitude towards life will enable you to overcome obstacles.

Finally remember those who have triumphed. Helen Keller, for example, who, although blind, deaf and dumb, achieved world fame as a lecturer and writer. And Stephen Hawking, despite developing a progressive nervous disease in his twenties, became a Cambridge professor and a leading authority in astro-physics. Of such this world is not worthy. And their indomitable spirit is available for all who want it. Let but the jaw set in resolve and the mind say *I will!* and all things are possible.

Disabled or not, go forward to claim your heritage – constant, radiant health.

New Words for the Taking

Inability to summon the appropriate word often means embarrassment. Such occasions will be reduced if you take steps to increase your vocabulary. You may claim a word is in your vocabulary if you are able to use it aptly and easily. To have a vague idea of its meaning is not enough.

No one is urging you to be a walking dictionary, but you will agree that a comprehensive vocabulary has many advantages. Not least is a fluency of expression which increases confidence. These, plus a pleasant voice and appearance, will earn you respect, open up opportunities for leadership and usher in significant and satisfying living.

Many people make do with a pitiably small stock of words. Their conversation crawls along as they mercilessly flog those colourless hacks – *sort of*, *I mean*, *you know*, *nice*, *got* and *funny*. If you want to increase your working vocabulary, the following procedures will help.

Develop a Liking for Words

Besides being useful, many words are beautiful, both in sound and appearance. For example, look at the list of precious stones in the twenty-first chapter of *Revelation*. Say them aloud, slowly, lovingly. Sample them critically, like a connoisseur delighting in favourite wines: *jasper*, *sapphire*, *chalcedony*, *emerald*, *sardonyx*, *chrysolite*, *beryl*, *topaz*, *chrysoprasus*, *jacinth*, *amethyst*.

Now pass on to *diaphanous, crystalline, hyacinth, tranquillity*. Look out for more and make a list of them. Revel in their sound and appearance.

Keep a Word-book

Carry a notebook in which to record every word that is new to you, or which you have to admit you could not have used confidently. It's useful to write down the phrase or sentence in which it occurs. In a few months you will have listed all the words you are likely to meet or require. Don't be dismayed if the list is formidable – it will yield to steady treatment. Once you become word-conscious, you will be surprised at your progress.

Here are a few for your first page: *parsimonious, irascible, vociferous, ubiquitous, surreptitious, euphemism*.

Learn a Daily Stint

Decide what your stint will be, say three to a dozen words. Transfer your stint to a larger book, writing the words down the left-hand side, and spacing them evenly. Now deal with each as follows. Consult a dictionary and check how the word is pronounced. Write the word several times, saying it aloud as you do so.

Next, concentrate on its meaning. Read the dictionary definition carefully. Then, if you wrote out the context in the first place, transfer this phrase or sentence to the larger book, deciding which meaning of the word was intended. Generally the first one or two meanings are the most common and important. Write these in your book, abbreviating or simplifying as necessary. Finally, frame the word in a short sentence of your own, and say this aloud several times as you write it.

Deal with each word of your stint in this way. You'll do three words in ten minutes or less, and you will really master them. Have a quick revision every week and month. In a year you will have increased your vocabulary appreciably.

Read Widely

Words are truly significant only in relation to other words. Reading not only introduces you to new words but shows you how to use them. It also keeps you familiar with those already met, and demonstrates how they have further meanings and uses. *Reading maketh a full man*, wrote Bacon, and it makes a full vocabulary, too. Authors differ in the extent of their vocabularies and each subject has its own specialized vocabulary. The more authors and subjects you read, the bigger your stockpile of words.

Study Groups of Words

Concentrate upon groups of words related to a particular subject or group of subjects, e.g. the sciences. Do you know with what the following are concerned? *Etymology, anthropology, philology, archaeology, geology.* Then there is a group of words concerned with words – *cliché, tautology, verbosity, simile, epigram, ambiguous, metaphorical, anticlimax.*

Another method is to take a prefix and consult a dictionary for its cognates. Thus *omni* (all) gives *omnipotence, omniscient, omnivorous. Mono* (one) gives *monogamy, monotone, monologue.* Now list words beginning with *bene-, poly-, uni-, ani-, magni-.*

This chapter is not meant to be a plea for the use of long words. Often the most profound speech and writing is couched in monosyllables. Only use long words when they convey your meaning more aptly than short ones. Often there is *one* word and *only one* which will do the job. A good vocabulary will enable you to use it.

The late G.A. Dorsey wrote:

> *Words are tools, the most amazing and important yet invented by the human brain. Lack of them may be as fatal to your progress in certain endeavours as leaden feet or untutored hands in others. Lack of knowledge of how to use words is as great a handicap to a writer or speaker as is ignorance of how to combine bricks and mortar to a mason.*

Increased Powers of Concentration

Ability to concentrate inevitably brings success. It gives mastery over situations, increases efficiency and enables you to solve your problems. Milton Wright says: 'The measure of a man is the extent to which he can concentrate.' Earlier, Emerson wrote: 'Concentration is the secret of success in politics, in war, in trade, in short in all the management of human affairs.'

If you feel your concentration is weak, be assured it is possible to improve it.

First, do all you can to shut out distractions. Studying in the living-room when the TV or radio is on or others are talking, is not helpful. Work alone and see the room is adequately ventilated, lighted and warmed. You must be unconscious of the body to give undivided attention.

As you begin, refuse to dream about the past or future. Don't let your eyes wander but keep them on your work. It will help if you write notes or draw sketches relevant to the subject. Resist any signs of self-pity.

One enemy of concentration is boredom. Your attention doesn't wander during an exciting film or when reading a gripping novel. Boredom may set in if you work for too long, so limit sessions to an hour; then take a ten-minute break and do something different.

You might use this time to stimulate your interest by recalling your original intentions and ambitions, and thinking of the rewards of success – greater security, interesting holidays, a better job. Make a list. It will act as a spur. 'Every man,' writes Brooks Atkinson, 'can achieve a great deal … according to the burning intensity of his will and the keenness of his imagination.'

Notice the first of these. You must *will to learn*. Much wandering attention is caused by half-hearted desire. If anything is worth learning it is worth learning thoroughly. Otherwise you will never be sure of your facts. Make up your mind to *master* the subject-matter and do not be content with a hazy smattering.

Avoid saying: 'I can't concentrate.' That is a negative suggestion and it is untrue. Instead, say: 'My concentration is improving.'

If you have difficulty in concentrating, you are not alone. We are all mentally lazy and will avoid thinking if we can. Knowing this, be ruthless with yourself. Flog yourself *mentally!* Don't be afraid of overworking – nothing will snap! Arnold Bennett maintained that we could tyrannize over the mind every hour of the day.

It will help if you set yourself a deadline. Give yourself a reasonable amount of work to be done in an hour, a week, a month. By thus giving yourself a challenge you enlist the aid of your emotions, and self-respect will goad you on.

You can devise further ways of strengthening concentration. Try totting up columns of figures. When you are proficient, do the same thing while the TV is on. As your concentration develops, speed and accuracy will be unaffected.

The final enemy of concentration is a spirit of defeatism. Never allow negative thoughts such as *I shall never master this.* Your brain is more able and versatile than you realize. Don't be afraid to stretch it. It will rise to heavier demands. Have confidence in your own powers. Attack the work with determination. In six months what now seems unintelligible will be understood.

A Much Improved Memory

A good memory is surely one of the essentials of successful living. A moment's thought will convince you of the many advantages it brings – increased efficiency, speedier acquisition of qualifications, promotion, popularity, more confidence in conversation and public speaking. There is also the freedom from regrets, humiliations and embarrassments caused by a poor memory.

Several fallacies exist regarding memory. The most widespread is that one may be endowed at birth with a 'bad' memory and that nothing can be done to improve it.

The fact is, the memory of every experience, everything we have heard or seen, is stored in the mind. A 'good' memory is the ability to recall at will any of those stored impressions. The following attitudes and practices will help you do this.

Stop Saying Your Memory is Bad

Declaring that one has a bad memory is a popular excuse for forgetfulness. It is the worst thing you can do if you want to improve it. Every time you say or think your memory is poor, you are making it so, for it is a psychological law that whatever is repeatedly suggested to the mind tends to become a reality.

To improve your memory, use this law positively. Suggest to yourself repeatedly, especially at night and as you wake in the morning, that your memory is improving.

Daily, as you adopt this positive attitude, and as you implement the following suggestions, your memory will get more and more reliable. The days when you had a poor memory are over. In future, every day will see an improvement.

Begin Trusting Your Memory

The invalid will never be strong again if he remains in bed. He must get up and *begin* to walk. Similarly, if you want your memory to get stronger, you must begin trusting it. Next time you go shopping, don't make a list, *trust your memory*.

To remember to do something, imagine yourself doing it at the time you wish to do it. For example, if you want to remember to take a book when you visit a friend tomorrow, see yourself now going out with the book under your arm. You will be surprised how quickly your memory becomes reliable. A few successful attempts at recall will be cumulative in their effect. You will trust your memory more confidently and with bigger tasks, and the more you do that, the better it will become.

Master Your Material

Make sure you completely understand the subject-matter you wish to memorize. Work at it until you have grasped every allusion and argument. If it is obscure, ask advice or consult a dictionary.

Another aid to understanding and recall is to make diagrams or sketches. A further useful practice is to explain the subject-matter to an imaginary pupil; preferably not a bright one!

Determine to Remember

We forget much because we do not determine to remember. We say, 'I *expect* I shall remember', or 'I *hope* I remember' or 'I'll *try* to remember.' We fail to make a definite act of the will –

'I *shall* remember.' With such half-hearted resolves, is it any wonder we forget? Next time you meet a stranger and want to remember his name, *will* to do so. In addition, associate his name with something or someone you know already.

Repetition

This time-honoured method of memorizing remains one of the most reliable. According to some authorities, repetition deepens the memory traces in the mind.

To repeat material aloud is more effective than doing it silently. Also, although parrot-like repetition helps recall, it is better to *think* about what you are repeating.

Numerous short periods of repetition are preferable to a few lengthy ones. The principle should be – *little and often*.

Avoid Dislike

Emotions play an important part in the learning process. We remember vividly every detail of personal triumphs or disasters when we were emotionally involved. If you allow yourself to dislike a subject, you will make slow progress and have difficulty in remembering the necessary facts. Children progress much better in subjects they like. Adults are the same. Things which have interested us are easily recalled. So the moral is – maintain interest and recall will be easy.

Learn Wholes Rather Than Parts

Experiments indicate that the best way to memorize a passage is to keep reciting it in its entirety rather than a few lines at a time. If the passage is long, divide it into sections and treat each as a unit.

Use Mnemonics

Mnemonics are useful, especially to examination candidates. Suppose, to answer a question adequately, you need to remember at least eight points. The first step is to summarize each point by one word. Next, write down the first letter of each of the eight words e.g. E, G, B, D, F, B, N, A. Finally, compose a sentence in which each word begins with one of these letters. Preferably make it humorous or nonsensical. *Every good boy deserves fruit but not apples* would do. Such a sentence easily lodges in the mind, and these initial letters will enable you to recall the necessary points.

Association

It seems that memory works rather like a conveyor belt, bringing up to the surface of the conscious mind any number of items provided that they are in some way connected.

One secret of a good memory lies in deliberately forging these chains of association. You link up the new material to be remember with something already so well known that there is no possibility of forgetting it. That begins the chain. Subsequently link up, in your mind, each item with its predecessor. When you want to recall, first call up the old, familiar item, and that will bring up the first of the new items, which will in turn recall the second and so on.

With regard to name-remembering, associate the new name or person with someone or something you are familiar with.

New Positive Emotions

Whether or not the whisk of mops is about your ears, to engage in *mental* spring-cleaning is always salutary. The cobwebs of bad habits, negative emotions and wrong attitudes make life a gloomy affair. Now is the time to swipe at them resolutely.

First, make for the black festoons of pessimism. Owing to several reverses you may have started thinking that *everything* will happen for the worst. 'No use going for a holiday,' you moan, 'it's sure to rain all the time.' 'No good trying for that job,' you say, 'I will never get it!' 'What me! Volunteer for that! I could never do it!'

Does that sound like you? Never trying, never hoping, never expecting any success or happy conclusion? You look for sickness and you get it; you're afraid of accidents and they come your way. Disappointments rain steadily upon you.

Allow this book to prompt you to snap out of this funereal attitude. Break with it, once and for all. In future, expect good things – success, health, advancement, prosperity. Displace despair by hope. Make war on negative thinking.

Perhaps for too long you have been regarding yourself as a pawn moved by some malicious fate. Now is the time to grasp firmly the reins of your own destiny. You have been pushed around by circumstances too long. From now on *you will control your circumstances!*

While lunging at pessimism, include also your tendency to worry and any feelings of inferiority. Worry is a waste of nervous energy. It accomplishes nothing, merely undermines your resilience and capacity to deal with the factors causing the trouble. Face your problems courageously, objectively. *Do something about them*, but refuse to worry.

Concerning feeling inferior, this is common. The *others* probably feel the same. This is because most people had experiences in infancy which made them feel weak, insignificant, foolish, ignorant, dirty or unloved. These memories and impressions, buried deep in the unconscious mind, go on exerting a baleful influence. At least, they will, unless you take steps to render them harmless.

You can do this as follows:

1. Try to recall any such humiliating childhood experiences. Get clues by recalling stories told in your family circle about your infancy.
2. Keep telling yourself that you refuse to allow childhood experiences to mar your adult life.
3. Always think and speak positively about yourself.
4. Speak reassuringly to yourself as you fall asleep, reminding yourself that you are, in fact, of worth, that you are accepted, respected and loved.
5. Dwell upon your uniqueness. No other person on the globe has qualities identical. Therefore you can make a contribution to life no one else can make – hence it is of extreme value. Rare things are always precious.

Be sure to sponge away all feelings of guilt. Guilty people are never completely happy. Ask others to forgive you, do all you can to make amends, and then forgive yourself.

Many guilty feelings spring from the sex impulse. They will evaporate if you accept your sex instinct as a normal part of your human make-up. It should not be a cause for self-reproach and consequent conflict.

While you're on this mental spring-cleaning, decide on some new furnishings within. Is it possible you have become completely selfish? If so, introduce a little unselfishness and thoughtfulness here and there. Do something to help others. Snap out of the imprisoning cell of self and begin living for other people. Resolve each day to make someone a little happier. How about getting involved in voluntary work? Acts like these let in peace, joy and sunshine. You become bigger, more sympathetic, more generous. You generate harmony within.

Talking of thoughtfulness, how about taking home a little present for your partner, or letting them know they are rather wonderful in an unspectacular way?

But thoughtfulness must extend outside the home. Are you thoughtful of your neighbours, your employees or employer? Do you co-operate with them as much as possible? Do you ever think about the people who make life easier for you – the road-sweeper, the postman, the office-cleaner, the dustman? They would be glad of a word of appreciation occasionally.

No spring-cleaning is complete without a 'blitz' on the windows. Dark curtains must come down. Grime must be washed from glass and paintwork. So with your mental spring-cleaning, the dark curtains of cynicism, bitterness and hatred must come down. Wash away the grime of negative emotions like jealousy, envy, the nursing of old wrongs. If you are religious, love God for all your worth and your neighbours as much as yourself – and that's a lot. If you're an atheist, still fulfil the second part of that ancient and sublime command. Open yourself to a generous love which will uplift and liberate. Then for you it will seem as if:

the winter is past,
the flowers appear on the earth,
and the time of the singing of birds has come.

An Attractive Voice and Clear Speech

The Importance of Good Speech

When you speak, do you mutter, or grunt, or whisper, or bellow? Are you understood first time? Is your voice attractive, or do others wince when you speak?

Good speech enhances personality. It will put you head and shoulders above the crowd, and may well pave the way for promotion and greater security.

Whether you like it or not, people judge you by your voice and the quality of your speech. If an employer is considering two applicants for a post or promotion, and they have the same qualifications, is it not likely that the better spoken one will be chosen?

Often speech is more important than personal appearance. Imagine two men who rise to speak in a public meeting. One is dressed like a tramp, but his speech is clear and forceful. He will command respect and attention despite his appearance. The other, immaculately dressed, speaks in a slovenly fashion and is barely audible. He will be largely ignored and probably dismissed as uneducated.

Undoubtedly your speech is your shop window. Dress it well and see that it attracts rather than repels.

Attractive speech is particularly important in view of the part played by the telephone in modern life. Over the wires your voice is your only commendation. You stand or fall by that alone. The very reputation of your firm may hang on the clarity and attractiveness of your voice. By that alone, courtesy, interest, pleasure, willingness and an impression of efficiency have to be conveyed.

In social life, although people are long-suffering, a clear, pleasant voice is a great asset. Coarse or indistinct speech endears us to few. And the monotonous speaker soon becomes a bore. Tiresome also are those who 'hum and haw', always at a loss for the right word, and their opposites who gabble like a torrent in full spate.

The human voice is capable of beautiful sound, even in daily speech. When so many sounds around you are raucous and ugly, why not begin taking a pride in the quality of your voice and speech?

The Causes of Poor Speech

Poor speech has two basic causes – environment and laziness. Once you *want* improvement, an unhelpful environment need no longer affect you detrimentally. Rather let it act as a goad to you to improve your speech.

The tongue and lips, like water, take the path of least resistance. Unless you determine otherwise, they will betray you. Your speech will continue to be, or may become, slovenly. With continued disuse, the muscles controlling the lips are unable to obey the call for action. Good speech becomes impossible.

Exercises to Improve Speech

Lax muscles of the lips, tongue and cheeks may be toned up in the same way as other muscles – by exercise. The easiest and most pleasant form is reading aloud. First, read several paragraphs loudly enough to be heard in a small hall. Next, repeat more slowly, stressing each syllable and over-emphasizing consonants, particularly initial and final ones.

You may think this sounds ridiculous, but persevere. A batsman practising strokes before a mirror looks ridiculous, but not when, as a result, he saves a match. The ballerina, likewise, spends countless hours in rigorous, self-disciplined exercise.

Another exercise for developing tone and resonance is to stand comfortably and take a deep breath. Then, with jaws clenched, read in a monotone, stressing each syllable equally until the breath is exhausted. Relax. Breathe again and read further in the same way. Hang on to each syllable for two seconds. Aim at strong, steady, vibrant sounds. Work through at least two paragraphs, then reread them aloud in the normal way. If the exercise has been done correctly, there will be an increased richness and resonance in the voice. This exercise sounds more ridiculous than the first, but it gives certain results.

A further exercise is to use the vowel sounds familiar to learners of shorthand and found in – *Pa, may we all go, too?* and *That pen is not much good.* Utter each vowel sound several times, prefacing it with a consonant; B and P, D and T, F and V are good ones to begin with. Stand as before, breathe deep, then, forming the lips carefully, make the sound suddenly, emitting air in the pent-up lungs so as to give an explosive effect. Thus:

Baa Bay Bee Ball Bo Boo

To develop muscles controlling the jaw and lips, work through the following, six times daily:

1. Push the lips forward in the whistling position; then bring back hard in an artificial grin.
2. Waggle the jaw sideways – like a cow chewing the cud!
3. Keep dropping the jaw down as far as it will go.
4. Repeat the words: *move, home, whistle, ran, down, torpid, apathetic.* Over-emphasize the movement of the lips.
5. Massage the cheeks.

The Constituents of Good Speech

Good speech implies clarity, variety of tone, and fluency. Aim at introducing these desirable elements into your speech.

Clarity comes when you enunciate vowels and consonants correctly and adequately, and is largely a matter of lip and tongue control. This comes only with practice.

Vowel sounds additional to those given above are found in – *bare*, *err*, *tie*, *toil*, *owl*, *bee*, *door*, *tour*. These words should be said daily, with great care, until you are sure you make them correctly in normal conversation.

The consonant sounds are indicated by capitals in the following words. These words also, and the consonants only placed before each of the vowels, should be repeated daily in the manner described. Be sure you make an *explosive* effect.

Pat	Goat	Lane	Wise	WHist
Bee	Five	Man	Yet	SHun
Tea	Vine	Name	CHoke	soNG
Done	So	Ran	THigh	baR
Cat	Zip	Hat	THine	

As you practise these sounds it is useful to watch your lip movements in a mirror.

Variety is the next requisite for good speech. Monotonous speech is deadly. Variety makes it interesting and attractive. Vary the pitch, speed, emphasis, volume and manner.

1. *Pitch*. Sometimes use high notes, sometimes low, and, of course, all those between. Say the following aloud: *What's the time in Australia, now? Are you coming tomorrow, Penelope?* It's almost impossible to say such sentences monotonously. Try to introduce these pleasant, lilting variations into everyday speech.

2. *Speed*. Vary the speed of your speech. Some people always speak slowly, others at a bewildering speed. Aim at a happy medium, with frequent excursions into the two extremes. Contrast the following:

> *The splendour falls on castle walls*
> *And snowy summits old in story.*
> *I chatter, chatter as I flow*
> *To join the brimming river.*

It is almost as impossible to say the first pair quickly as the second slowly. Thus reading poetry aloud is excellent for inducing variety of speed to say nothing of other variations.

3. *Emphasis*. The importance of emphasis is obvious if you say the following sentence six times, stressing a different word each time: *Did he lend you twenty pounds?* Make use of the simple device of emphasis to brighten your speech. It will also help you to hold attention and drive home a point. These are essentials for effective speaking either in conversation or from the platform. The reading of plays aloud is also useful in this connection.

4. *Volume*. Variation in the volume or strength of your voice is also desirable, and at all times it must be appropriate. What you say may be scintillating, but it will be lost if it is not heard. Make sure you do not drop your voice at the end of sentences.

5. *Manner*. Be sure you put emotional values into your voice. The same sentence may be said sadly, scornfully, incredulously, fiercely, light-heartedly and so on. Pull out *all* the stops. Cultivate, for the most part, a cheerful, hopeful voice which reveals friendliness, sincerity and sympathy.

The third factor in good speech is fluency. This comes with a plentiful supply of ideas and an adequate vocabulary. These lead to confidence which in turn improves fluency. Needless to say, the organs of speech must be kept in trim. Reading aloud for ten minutes several times a week will ensure this, once they are in good condition. In his excellent book *Successful Living*, the late Dr Beran Wolfe writes:

> *Practise reading the the works of the better authors aloud. The fine art of reading aloud ... has fallen into decay because it is so much easier to listen to the radio than to cultivate a good speaking voice ... As a psychologist, I cannot impress upon you too seriously the importance of the development of speech as a means towards successful living.*

General Hints

Sincerity and friendliness will put charm into your voice, and this will be augmented as you cultivate a real interest in people.

Avoid sarcasm, irony, bitterness, impatience, anger and pride. These make the voice harsh, bitter, cold or lifeless.

Engaging in amateur dramatics is an interesting way of developing confidence and improving quality and resonance in the voice. Another is listening carefully to good speakers. Become speech conscious.

Above all, seize every opportunity of speaking in public. Asking questions from the floor is a good way for the nervous to start.

An attractive voice quickly ceases to be so if its owner lacks the ability to speak about a variety of subjects. The person with the one-track mind, enthusiast though he may be, quickly loses his appeal to those who do not share his interest. Be sure, then, to develop wide interests, and keep acquainted with current events and trends.

More Tact Tomorrow

Day in, day out, marriages are wrecked, jobs are lost, hearts are broken – all for want of tact. This subtle, highly desirable quality is the very lubricant of living. With it the wheels of life turn smoothly; without it all is discord and friction.

What exactly is tact? Essentially it is a thoughtfulness or consideration for others which steers us through life – hurting, humiliating, inconveniencing others as little as possible.

The tactless person leaves a trail of wounded spirits – people who are smarting, crushed or angry through contact with him. No one who does that may call their life successful, however much money they have made. What's more, the person who is always making others unhappy is bound, sooner or later, to be made unhappy themselves.

Tact is easy to develop. It's merely a matter of doing, or refraining from doing, certain things.

Situations to Avoid

First consider tact in its negative aspect.

1. *Avoid making people look small.* No one likes being humiliated – even the most humble person. The natural reaction is resentment, anger, dislike, perhaps hatred.

   Mrs X was tactless in this way. Strangely enough, the victim of her tactlessness was her husband whom she continually decried before friends. Actually she had a wonderful husband, but no one ever heard a word of praise or appreciation from Mrs X.

24

Learn from this woman. Unless it is your job to do so, avoid drawing attention to the shortcomings of others; where possible throw a cloak over them. Be generous and understanding in your assessment of others' behaviour. Give them the benefit of any doubt. Others, like yourself, are proud and sensitive, and hold themselves in esteem.

If in your work you are expected to spot inefficiency and rebuke others, do so without giving offence. First find something to commend. The culprit will then accept adverse criticism without sulking. That way, he is more likely to amend his ways.

2. *Avoid infringing the rights of others*. People have rights which they guard jealously. If, tactlessly, you infringe those rights without consulting them, there is bound to be trouble.

Everyone has a right to a private life, so avoid pumping for information. In attempting to make conversation, don't let your questions become too personal.

At home, remember that others have a right to privacy. Couples should remember this, and parents in regard to teenage children. Rooms should not be entered without a knock, nor drawers rummaged through without warning.

Young Mr K loved his wife and so prided himself that she kept no secrets from him that he would open her letters. Such tactlessness annoyed his wife intensely, but she said nothing for fear of hurting his feelings and arousing suspicion.

Similarly tactless is the girlfriend who is asked to stay behind for a drink after work and doesn't think to call her partner to let him know she will be late home.

3. *Avoid boosting yourself.* Blowing your own trumpet does not win you respect or popularity. If you *must* mention your own accomplishments, do so modestly and in a lighter vein. Not to do so is tactless because it tends to make others small by implication.

4. *Don't teach other people their jobs.* Even a roadsweeper is professionally proud. He is convinced he knows his job 'inside out', and that no one can teach him anything about it. He will resent anyone trying.

   Jim was the best apprentice of his year but he lacked tact. He hadn't been in his job a fortnight before he tried to alter a process his foreman had introduced ten years before. That Jim had ideas was to his credit. It was the crude way he put them forward which caused trouble and ruined his chances.

Kindness and Consideration

Now for the more positive aspects of tact.

It is tactful to make people feel at ease. This is always appreciated. You will know what to do and say if you place yourself imaginatively in the other's place.

It is tactful to show appreciation of services done on your behalf. Do this sincerely and not in a cursory way.

It is tactful to make others feel important. We are all born egotists. People thrive on praise and the assurance that they are needed and doing a worthwhile job. During the Second World War, the rate of sickness in one unit was reduced to one-tenth once it was brought home to the personnel that the monotonous job they were doing was making a vital contribution to victory.

Be liberal, then, with praise and appreciation. That does not mean flattery and the smooth tongue. Look for things to praise and you will find them. Everyone has good points.

It is tactful to be courteous at all times and to all people. Rudeness and brusqueness seldom pay. In other words, show deference to people, remembering that they are not 'inferiors' or 'hands' or 'public servants', but individuals.

Tact also shows itself in respecting what others hold dear, particularly religion, politics, race and family. Anything which another feels deeply about must be treated with understanding and sympathy.

Life offers a thousand situations where a little tact will act as oil in machinery. For example, it is tactful to be punctual. If you feel you have made some mistake, it is tactful to acknowledge it immediately and apologize.

When you make a phone call, you are, quite uninvited, thrusting yourself into someone's home or business. Suddenly you are making a demand upon someone's time and attention. It is tactful, therefore, to apologize for the intrusion; you do not know what activity you may have interrupted.

It is tactful not to defy convention deliberately. People who attend a formal dinner casually dressed let themselves down badly, annoy fellow guests and embarrass the host.

Another sign of tact is to avoid monpolizing conversation. Other people like to talk as well as yourself, so give them a chance. Particularly if you are a newcomer to a group, beware of being too talkative.

It is obvious from the foregoing that to be more tactful is a certain way of living harmoniously with your fellows.

STEP 8

Giving Your Boss a Better Deal

Being human, your employer wants value for money, with the best people in the key positions of the business. The best people are those who give most for the company's money. Impress your boss in the following ways.

Always be Conscientious

Consistent lateness is daylight robbery. You are paid to be at your post for certain hours. See you are there.

Secondly, don't waste company materials either by bad workmanship or using them for your own purposes.

Thirdly, don't waste time. Avoid gossiping, making private phone-calls, doing personal jobs, extending lunch and tea breaks, and leaving before time.

Lastly, do your work to the best of your ability. Your employer expects that from you. You were engaged on that assumption. Shoddy, third-rate work is a form of pilfering.

Improve Yourself in Every Way

Dress appropriately for the job. Look tidy and clean to start the day, even if your work entails getting dirty.

Improve your speech. No matter what your job, this will help you. People judge you by the way you speak. If your speech is clear and attractive, it will help to mark you out for promotion.

Extend your general education. In many situations, a good general education will place you head and shoulders above your colleagues.

Take an Interest in Your Work

Find out why you do what you do. Know something of the history of your job, your trade or profession, your firm. Visualize its future development.

See your particular work in relation to the ultimate objective or finished product. Think how your work is contributing to the welfare of others.

Ask questions concerning your job. You may hit upon some idea for improvement and progress. Questions reveal not so much ignorance as an enquiring mind.

Most important, seriously consider studying for further qualifications. In this day of fierce competition, there is little chance of advancement without them.

Be Willing

Employers like folk who are willing to undertake new work, new responsibilities, or who are willing to do something extra to their duties. Willing people make the lot of the business executive so much easier. They ensure the success of any enterprise. They enhance their own value.

Be Cheerful

Cheerfulness is allied to willingness, and is equally valued by employers.

Promotion will go to the cheerful rather than to the moaning employee. Cheerfulness makes you likeable. It puts people on your side and paves the way for advancement.

Watch Human Relationships

Try to keep on good terms with everyone at your place of employment. You will then be doing your share to keep the organization running smoothly and happily.

This will work in your favour also. If you are known to get on well with people, it will be a point to your advantage when promotions are being considered. You are hardly likely to be put in charge of others if it is thought you would upset them and cause them to resign. The biggest factor in maintaining good relationships is tact, and this is dealt with in Step 7.

Keep Relaxed

Taut, strained employees are not the most efficient. They tend to make mistakes, ruin relationships and go on the sick-list. Therefore, work hard on the job, but don't take its problems home with you. You'll do better work on duty if you have a complete change when you're off. You will keep fitter, too. Every day you are away ill you are a complete loss to your employer.

Like Your Work

You will never do good work in a job you hate. If you are in that unfortunate position, either change your job or your attitude to it.

To do the latter, carry out the suggestions already given. Further, think of the advantages of your job – the security it gives you, the essentials of life it enables you to buy, the contribution it makes to human life and happiness. Dwell on these rather than on its disadvantages. Remember, too, that no job is ideal in every way.

As a further help, try auto-suggestion. Repeat the following jingle to yourself as you fall off to sleep each night:

My job appears each passing day
To be more pleasing every way.

It's well worth while cultivating a liking for your job. Day by day you will go to it eager, fresh and happy. *To such people promotion comes inevitably.*

Towards Improved Ideals

This world needs people with ideals. Too many drift through life having no standard and no ideals to beckon them forward.

Ideals are an essential for progress. They goad us out of lethargy and self-complacency. If some people had not been idealists we should still be clothing ourselves with skins. The inventor and the reformer keep the clock of progress ticking.

You may not claim to be in either of these categories, but you will find it helpful to have your own ideals.

Firstly, hold the ideal of perfect health for yourself. Don't be content to limp through life dogged by constant ailments. Don't be like the people who expect poor health and who get it! Be sure to read the first chapter of this book again.

Next, be an idealist regarding your own personality. Aim at completeness, harmonious development – in a word, maturity. Jesus of Nazareth encouraged people to be idealists. 'Be ye perfect,' He is recorded to have said, 'even as your Father in heaven is perfect.'

Too many people are content to remain undeveloped and childish in their emotions, reactions and characteristics. Some will pride themselves upon their fiery temper, forgetting that when they were young such outbursts were called tantrums. Others will become bullies in the office whenever something isn't going their way, failing to recognize they are acting like a spoilt child.

Many adults retain the arrogance of youth, with its intolerance, impatience and lack of understanding. Some remain entirely egocentric like small children; they never look beyond the confines of their own hopes and desires.

To keep before you the ideal of a full-orbed character will act as an incentive and impel you forward towards maturity. Don't rest content while you can find within yourself any traces of the juvenile. Cultivate patience, tolerance, understanding. Develop always the wide view, broad sympathies and generous interpretation.

Self-knowledge will help you towards this ideal. To be able to recognize the different ingredients of your own human make-up will increase your self-mastery, and keep you from the snap judgment or uncharitable condemnation.

Thirdly, be an idealist regarding your mind. Be ambitious to keep it keen, sensitive and aware. There is much around you to encourage coarseness and lethargy, so cultivate an ear and eye for what is good and beautiful. Seek only the best in the arts. Observe the wonders and beauties of nature – the ever-changing pageant of the skies, the fragrance of flowers, the grace of trees, the innocence of children, the laughing eyes of a girl in love. Look, too, for beauty in the characters of others – unselfishness, courage, patience, cheerfulness, sympathy.

If you don't already love it, turn again to poetry. Forget your youthful prejudices and make a genuine attempt to enjoy it. Remember, it should be read aloud; and you will appreciate a poem only when you understand its every reference. A poet is especially sensitive to beauty, and more aware than most of what is going on around him. If you tarry with him, he cannot but improve the quality of your mind.

Not only poetry but the prose works of the élite of the ages will refine the mind. A knowledge of history, too, will make its own contribution.

Your commonsense will tell you that there are some areas of life where the pursuit of an ideal might cause distress and unhappiness.

The first is in marriage. Never expect your partner to measure up to your ideal. Paragons do not exist. You must expect to find failings in your partner. It is just possible you have a few yourself!

Secondly, never expect your employment to be ideal in every respect. There are snags in the best of jobs. Those who would not change their work if they could, admit this.

Thirdly, don't expect to find a place to live where everything comes up to your dreams. Instead, concentrate on those aspects which satisfy you and forget the others.

With these exceptions, there *is* a place for idealism in life so long as you do not become a perfectionist. Such people are unrealistic and unhappy. Most important: confine your ideals to your own behaviour and activities, and do not demand them of others.

Make Maturity Your Goal

'He's a person of mature judgment' – 'She shows a maturity of taste beyond her years.' Doubtless you would feel complimented to hear such remarks about yourself.

Yes, maturity is a coveted condition: it increases your prestige, your value as a citizen and your charm as a person. It does much to make life serene, constant and happy.

Maturity should come naturally with the years, but often it doesn't except in the physical sense. We have all met the person advanced in years who shows the emotional characteristics of childhood or adolescence.

Miss X had a shed littered with past 'crazes' – hobbies with which she had spent time and money only to forsake them after a few months. To flit from interest to interest, never to pursue anything for long is a characteristic of childhood. It should not be found in an adult.

Mr M is an efficient person in his late forties who holds a responsible post. In some ways he *is* mature, but in the matter of his religion he has never moved from those beliefs which satisfied him as an adolescent.

Mr Y, a former executive, shows immaturity in his retirement. Like a spoilt child he refuses to do anything to amuse himself or to help others. He spends most of his money on cigarettes, regardless of the financial embarrassment of his children upon whom he has thrust himself, and whose lives he dominates from his armchair. Such thoughtless selfishness and refusal to accept responsibilities may be tolerated in the young; with the old it is inexcusable.

Immaturity is a common condition. We all recognise the man in middle life who expects his wife to 'mother' him as his mother had done. Then there is the woman who holds political views with the narrow intolerance of a teenager.

With a view to increasing your own maturity, give careful thought to the following:

Prejudice

It is easy to see that this word means judgment before all the facts are known. Many of us jump to hasty conclusions. It is a mark of maturity to withhold judgment until all the facts are known.

Prejudice is unfair to others and to yourself. It may mean others suffering an injustice; it may keep you from the truth.

Superstition

If you are mature, you will have no time for superstitions. In fact, you enjoy 'knocking them for six'. You will walk under a ladder with a mischievous grin. Should you find that thirteen sit down for dinner, you are unperturbed. You recognize that superstitions are a legacy of the past when ignorance and illogical thinking were rife. Knowledge and sane thinking now free you from the fears and restrictions that superstitions would impose.

Ignorance

The mature person is ignorant of many things, but knows it. The immature person is ignorant of many things, but *doesn't* know it! The former is always seeking to extend his knowledge, detesting the one-track mind and the parochial outlook.

His bookshelves reveal wide interests. The mature person is informed about the past and hopeful of the future, appreciating that although the progress of mankind is slow, the overall picture is one of steady advance.

Fear

In acquiring maturity you seek to eradicate fear from your life. Rather than fearing your fellows, you show an interest in them. You try to understand *why* they behave as they do; the whole bent of your life is towards helping them. You have discovered that *perfect love casts out fear*.

As a mature person you have no fears about your health. Leading a temperate life, you will have good relationships with others, plus refusing to worry has brought you to a state of good health in which you are confident you will remain.

You do not fear for your future; you have taken what steps you can to provide for it. For the rest, you have sufficient confidence in yourself – and in life – to know there is no cause for anxiety. You can face even death unafraid. You have faced the fact that it is inevitable. Secondly, you are either convinced that death is the end, or it is the doorway to a new and exciting existence. In either event there is nothing to fear.

More positively, a mature person is generally found to possess the following qualities:

Tolerance

As a mature person you regard everyone as your brother or sister regardless of colour, creed or status.

You accept that there is more than one way of looking at every question; laying no claim to a monopoly of the truth. Your motto is 'Live and let live!' You know that here are few evils which do not contain some good and that Man quickly contaminates truth with error. Maturity keeps you from being over-confident, dogmatic, conceited or proud.

Consideration

When you have reached maturity of mind, you are not so pre-occupied with yourself as to be regardless of the comfort and feelings of others. Maturity allows you to put yourself imaginatively in the place of others and react accordingly. You are big enough to do this.

Detachment

Maturity enables you to view a situation impartially and unselfishly. A mature attitude to life is like that of an adult at a children's party – happy in their happiness, and willing to lose, to be overlooked, if it furthers the interests and happiness of others.

Even with your own abilities, as a mature person you can assess them impartially. You don't allow prowess in any sphere to fly to your head; neither do you engage in mock modesty.

Constancy

A mature person is constant, reliable, and master of their moods. Being mature, you possess powers of 'stickability' and are not deterred by difficulties. You are prepared to work for distant objectives, things which may not materialize for years.

Cheerfulness

A mature person keeps cheerful because they don't take themselves too seriously. A mature person can be reprimanded and not sulk, and can lose with good grace. Above all, you will shun self-pity and take full responsibility for your actions and not look for scapegoats.

Absence of Negative Emotions

No one may be called mature if they bear grudges or allow hatred to fester within. Neither is a person mature if they indulge in jealousy, envy or meanness.

These are the characteristics you must develop if you make maturity your goal.

Happier Relationships Ahead

Countless homes are wrecked and countless children suffer heartbreak because so many couples fail to make a success of their relationship.

Read this chapter even if you are single – it may help you to build a successful relationship one day. If you *are* happily married or living with your partner, it may mean even greater happiness; if your relationship is going on the rocks, it may save that catastrophe.

What is the secret of a happy relationship? Surely it is an adequate realization by each partner of the needs of the other, and an imaginative and determined effort to meet them.

Take the everyday chores of cooking, cleaning, laundering and maintenance of your home. You should not begrudge the time and effort involved in carrying out such household chores. Do not assume that your partner will do all the work around the house. You should both take responsibility. If a busy work-load makes this difficult, consider hiring a cleaner to reduce some of the burden for your partner. Otherwise, your partner will become resentful and think you are taking advantage of them.

We all need to feel appreciated and to have constant reassurance of our partner's love. And this should be demonstrated not only with obvious endearments but by actions which show thought and consideration. Remember how much your partner enjoys breakfast in bed or a massage after a stressful day, and now and again some flowers or a small gift.

There is also the universal desire to escape at times. Both must recognize this need in the other and see that it is met. This is where recreation, outside interests, 'treats' and holidays come in. There *must* be periodic breaks from the humdrum and routine.

So if it's three months since you went to the cinema or out for a meal together, it's time you did something about it. You don't want your relationship to become stale and predictable, do you? Every relationship needs a bit of variety.

If your partner seeks escape in some craft or pursuit, don't begrudge them this personal time or get irritated at the mess they make. They'll be a happier, more contented partner for that hobby. Rather, take an interest in it, ask questions about it, drop a word of praise or appreciation occasionally. By the way, your partner would think you were just wonderful if you bought them some little tool or accessory connected with their hobby.

Another primary need is to be noticed, admired, liked. If your partner begins to ignore your good qualities, and so far forgets themselves as to belittle you before friends or the children, they have only themselves to blame if you look else-where for praise and attention.

It is important to realize that moving in together or a marriage ceremony should not destroy the need for admira-tion. We all like to be told as much *now* that we are attractive and look charming or that a new outfit or hair-style suits us as we did when we first started dating. Also, do not allow yourself to become so selfish and thoughtless as not to notice the many things your partner does for you, the home and the children. And let them *know* that you have noticed what they are doing.

Both man and woman should continue to take a pride in their appearance, ensuring always that they are clean and well groomed. Try and maintain the same standard you set when you first started dating.

Many troubles spring from unsatisfactory sexual relationships. It is doubtful if any relationship has foundered where there has been a recognition on both sides of the sexual needs of the other and a genuine, unrestrained effort made to meet them. In many cases that effort is never made. Many people still find it very difficult to talk about sex with their partner, then wonder why they have become dissatisfied.

Ignorance on either side of the physiological and psychological aspects of sexual relationships is unnecessary today when so many reliable books on the subject are widely available. If you have any fears or doubts, look for reassurance in one of these guides.

The Master Key

A sure panacea for relationship trouble and the master key to marital bliss is the simple and obvious one of mutual consideration. To develop this, let each place himself imaginatively in the place of the other. It is then merely a question of asking yourself how you would feel in those circumstances and how you would like the other to behave towards you. Then, of course, there must be ACTION.

The cultivation of humility and a sense of humour are important. Likewise, that each learns to accept faults, failures and foibles as part of the other's personality and be big enough to go on loving.

STEP 12

Better Communications

Conversation and addressing groups are the two main forms of communicating with others. For both, you need a fair measure of self-confidence. If, naturally, you lack this, you will find it develops as you practise the principles advocated in this book. In particular, you should:

(a) Recollect instances from your childhood which humiliated you, and then 'laugh them out of court'. Why should you allow something which happened in infancy to continue to affect your adult life?
(b) Accept yourself as a person of worth. Esteem yourself, value yourself. Rejoice in your own uniqueness. And because you are unique, remember that you can make a contribution to life which no one else can make.
(c) Constantly remind yourself that you have a great untapped potential of ability.
(d) Fill up any gaps in your general education.
(e) Improve the quality of your voice and speech (see Step 6).

Given self-confidence, the next step towards improving conversation is a genuine liking for others. You will find this comes as you carry out (b) above. In the wake of this liking for others will come a 'disinterested interest' in them, and this will make it easy for you to draw them out in conversation. Few people are loath to talk about themselves, their interests and activities. Your interest in them as people will make it easy for you to discover their favourite subjects. Strike such a 'gusher' and

43

your conversational problems are solved. An occasional question or comment is all that is required to maintain the flow.

But good conversation should be more than a one-sided diatribe, and contributions should come from all the group. Further, by looking at the subject from various angles, it should be possible to keep on it for some time and not to hop from subject to subject like blackbirds on a lawn.

Certain phrases stimulate conversation, and they are worth remembering. *How do you feel about ...? What's your opinion of ...?* Often the simple interrogatives inject fresh life into a flagging conversation, especially *Why?*

It is an advantage in conversation to have thought through to your own convictions about all major issues. Some knowledge of history and the sciences, however superficial, is a help; also an acquaintance with current books, films, plays and events.

As much as possible, speak with feeling and enthusiasm. Avoid droning and hardly moving your lips as if you aspire to be a ventriloquist. So many speak in a 'deadpan' voice which lacks feeling, life and interest. When you speak with confidence, zest and sparkle, your personality shines through, and you make more impact.

Remember to take an interest in words; the more you have at your disposal the better you will converse (see Step 2). Finally, avoid using hackneyed expressions, and making trite, obvious remarks.

The ability to address groups of people is a most satisfying form of self-expression, seeing that it meets the basic need to be significant. Anyone of average intelligence may become an acceptable public speaker.

Naturally you must be audible, so train yourself to speak with clarity and vigour, stressing important words and making effective use of pauses. Given clear speech, a reasonable command of language, and ideas or a message you wish to impart, you will need to observe the following:

1. *Prepare well.* Preparation for public speaking may be direct or indirect. Under the latter comes wide reading, observation, deep thought and a general sense of awareness. Direct preparation involves getting a firm grasp of your subject, brooding over it, getting to know far more than you are going to use.

   Next, gather all relevant material likely to be of interest to your audience. Place this under suitable headings, each of which should lead naturally to the next. When you have ample material, select only the best, bearing in mind the type of audience you are going to face.

   At this stage, some speakers write out their speech in full. This is useful – to start with, at least – provided you do not allow your language to become stilted or bookish. And make no attempt to learn what you have written by heart. Instead, use it to make a summary on two or three postcards. Use these cards for rehearsing your speech. Do not worry about using the same words each time. Remember to take these cards with you and do not try to conceal them from your audience – they are no disgrace. Later, with more experience and confidence, you will be able to memorize your main points, and then you can dispense with notes.

2. *Your appearance and delivery.* Be well groomed but not over-dressed. Err on the side of the conventional. If possible, begin with a smile or at least a pleasant expression. Your audience will not expect you to look depressed or worried.

Stand erect and appear relaxed and confident. For the most part stand still but an occasional shift in position is not distracting.

Beginners are often troubled about what to do with their hands. The best advice is to forget them. Get so gripped by what you are saying and with the desire to make an impact on your audience that your hands will take care of themselves. Until you get into that state, let your hands hang loosely by your sides, whence they will easily swing into natural gestures; though beware of an indefinite waving of the hands which means nothing. When you find yourself using a gesture, let it be a definite one.

If you are unable to rest your notes on a table, hold them in one hand so as to leave the other free for gestures.

Generally, direct your gaze just over the heads of those sitting in the middle, but occasionally take everyone into its orbit. Avoid looking at the floor, ceiling or windows.

3. *Platform nerves*. Even experienced speakers get nervy just before speaking, so you must expect it. It will help you to keep controlled, however, if you keep yourself feeling friendly towards your audience. Remember it consists not of enemies, but good, kindly folk who have paid you a compliment by coming along to listen to you.

This feeling of friendliness will enhance your sincerity, and give your voice qualities which will help your listeners to like you in return. Bear this in mind then – *while you are loving an audience you cannot be scared of it.*

Also keep relaxed and breathe deeply. Regard the tendency to be nervy as nature's way of preparing you to be your best.

4. *Be vital.* Call on your own experiences as much as possible. This will enable you to be more graphic and to fill in colourful and precise details.

To gain and hold interest, make what you say in some way directly connected with the best interests of the audience. Your opening remarks, in particular, should be carefully chosen to 'whet the appetite'.

Use concrete words rather than abstract. For example, it is better to say *The sun jabbed into my spine like a gimlet* rather than *I found the heat extremely trying*.

What was said above about vocabulary applies especially to the public speaker. You must have a large stock of words upon which you may call promptly and confidently. The ready use of the right word leads to fluent, convincing, colourful speech.

5. *Be enthusiastic.* Your attitude towards your subject will largely determine that of your audience. If you are placid or indifferent, your audience will be the same. Speak with fervour, feeling, enthusiasm, and you will quickly have your audience reflecting the same qualities. With enthusiasm, the most crude of speakers makes an impact on an audience; without it, the words of the most accomplished are largely ineffective.

Getting More From Your Reading

You are wise if you learn to love books. 'A good book,' says Milton, 'is the life-blood of a master spirit.' When we read such a book we are contacting a mind more sensitive and aware than our own, and such an experience is stimulating and beneficial, lifting us into new worlds of thought and experience.

There are many reasons why we cannot entertain such authors into our homes to bask in their brilliance and wit, but a book enables us to enjoy their versatility whenever we wish. The printed word robs time, distance and death of their sting.

Many centuries have passed since Marcus Aurelius first thought aloud to his amanuensis. Yet in your sitting-room you may hear him say: *Our life is what our thoughts make it.* Over a century has passed since Charles Lamb left his desk at India House for the last time, but you may enjoy his quiet leg-pulling whenever you take down a copy of *Elia*. In such ways books tap the wisdom and wit of the centuries and bring them within reach of your armchair.

Respect for books changes to affection as you become familiar with them. You come to regard favourite books as old friends. You turn to them expectantly when you need diversion or inspiration. You open them at favourite passages and revel in them again. Thus you become a lover of books.

Obviously you need to possess some of your own. A humble shelf of secondhand ones will do, though it would whet your appetite to buy yourself a new book once a week or month. Having your own books has advantages: you are free to mark them as you will; fly-leaves may be used to index favourite passages under suitable headings. You also have the joy of lending books. You will lose some, but that is better than being a literary miser. Keep your books circulating, scattering knowledge, inspiration and pleasure.

Acquiring Literary Taste

So much printed matter pours from the presses every day that you must learn to discriminate in your reading. You must develop a taste for the best. How is this acquired?

Concentrate first on the accepted classics, books which have stood the test of time, the critical judgment of generations. This will demand patience, effort and concentration, but it is time well spent. The classics will lift you to their level and you will soon find yourself rejecting trashy literature. Suppose you began with an historical thriller – Charles Reade's *The Cloister and the Hearth*. Then you might go on to George Eliot's *Silas Marner* and then to *Jane Eyre*, *Pickwick Papers*, *The Vicar of Wakefield* and *Tess of the d'Urbervilles*. Later you could tackle some more modern classics like Conrad, Forster, Barrie, Priestley and Mary Webb.

Such reading works quietly, like leaven. Spend the leisure time of one year with such books and you will have the experience of scales dropping from your eyes. You will be conscious of new glories in the world around you. You will have a new interest in people. You will find yourself feeling more acutely, being bigger in spirit, wiser, more tolerant.

Remember, if we fail to appreciate a classic, the fault lies with ourselves. We are in the presence of a mental superior. If we find him dull it is because *we* are too obtuse to enjoy his wit, too dull to appreciate his subtlety.

Do not expect violent pleasure or *slapstick* from a classic. We must allow the author to lift us to his level, not expect him to descend to ours. And don't be in such a hurry that you have no time to *think* about what you are reading. Only in this way will you receive the full enrichment a book is waiting to bestow.

'People who would sooner hibernate than feel intensely,' wrote Arnold Bennett, 'will do well to eschew literature.'

How to Use Books

Books offer amusement, knowledge, wisdom, inspiration, challenge. Whatever you seek from a book will determine your treatment of it. If you want amusement or escape, read in a relaxed position. As you settle down, say to yourself, 'I'm going to enjoy this.' Then, when you find something which gives you pleasure, read it again and relish it to the full.

If it's knowledge you are after, set out to *master* the book. Tackle it in a businesslike fashion. Sit upright at a table with pen and notebook. If the book is your own, mark the key sentences in each paragraph. Read each chapter at least twice and then write out the gist of it in your own words.

Before studying a book it is well to read the preface. The author probably has something important which he wants you to know. Next, with a non-fiction book, read the chapter headings. And remember you are not bound to read the whole of a book, nor the chapters in order. Go straight to the chapters which interest you.

How Fast Do You Read?

A reasonable speed for average material is about 300 words a minute. Some people can read at more than double that speed. With practice it is possible for plodders to increase their speed. The secret lies in not saying *each* word mentally. Instead, look ahead and extract the meaning from phrases by seeing them as wholes or units. Progress by *seeing*, not by 'speaking inaudibly'. This is the way we read a slogan on a hoarding. We take it in all at once. It takes considerable practice to master this technique but it is a skill well worth acquiring.

By the way – don't say you have no time for reading. Put aside a mere fifteen minutes a day and though but an average reader, you will get through at least twenty books in a year!

Problems are for Solving

You can't expect to go through life without meeting problems; difficulties, perplexities, frustrations are an inevitable part of human experience. Accept this idea of the inevitability of problems; it will help you approach them in a robust frame of mind rather than thinking you are a victim specially singled out by a malignant fate.

While accepting the inevitability of problems, avoid a spirit of defeatism or pessimistic fatalism. You may have to face problems, but that does not mean that you are to be helpless in their throes, tossed about like a cork on the ocean.

Courage, clear thinking and faith will enable you to negotiate the stormy seas of life, and the experience will make you wiser and maturer. You will not have succumbed to your problems; rather they will have made a contribution to your development.

When confronted with a problem, the first thing to do is to gather all relevant data. Get acquainted with all the facts of the case. Then write down exactly what the problem is, state it simply in black and white. This gives you something definite with which to come to terms. The enemy is assessed and you are no longer fighting a nebulous body whose very indefiniteness worries you.

Next, give serious thought to the problem. Make sure that such thought does not degenerate into worry. Worry accomplishes nothing. Aim at clear, dispassionate thought. View the problem as if it were a friend's and not your own. Look at it from all angles and from the viewpoint of all concerned. You court disaster if you are entirely selfish in your outlook.

The problem examined broadly and impartially, write down all the possible solutions or courses of action. The knowledge that you have done this will keep you from useless regrets later, when you can remind yourself that all possible courses were examined and you took what appeared to be the best.

Having drawn up your list of possible solutions, weigh them impartially. Again bear in mind the claims and reactions of all concerned. Ruthlessly delete courses which would harm other people or cause you twinges of conscience. Act in accordance with the highest ideals. No step is a solution if later it is going to burden you with feelings of guilt or self-reproach.

Next, eliminate all proposed solutions which are seen on further thought to be impracticable.

You will now find that your list has been whittled down to two or three possibilities. At this stage it is often a good plan to get out into the open air. Go for a walk or ride, preferably somewhere with wide horizons. There, out in the open, review the problem afresh. You will find it appears much less formidable. And ask yourself how the difficulty will appear in ten years' time, or even one! Now turn to the remaining solutions and, before you return home, decide which you are going to adopt.

As you go to sleep that night, let your last thoughts be upon your decision. If, in the morning, you still feel it is the best one to take, go ahead.

If you have a friend you think is capable of giving sound advice, consult them. Do this before you go further, so you have the benefit of their views before you decide. Talking things over with another is always a great help. It enables you to isolate the problem and to decide which are the important factors. Even though the friend offers no advice, a sympathetic ear will help you. Further, as you describe to your friend the courses open to you, you will see them in a clearer light. Some will appear impossible even while you speak. Alternatively, one will appear most attractive.

Having decided on a course of action and carried it out, avoid useless regrets. Hold on to the thought that you looked into the matter thoroughly and carried out what seemed at the time the best solution.

Your problem may be of a kind where you need professional guidance from a solicitor, doctor, marriage-guidance counsellor or minister of religion. Any of these will be willing to help you. Some will require a fee, but the saving in anxiety and nervous energy will make it well worthwhile.

Another possible source of help may be one of the magazines or papers which contain a 'problem page'. Such services are reliable and generally free or at a nominal cost only.

In dealing with problems, remember the time factor. Some get more complicated the longer they are left. Get to grips with these immediately. Other problems solve themselves in time, and delaying tactics are the best form of action.

Reasonable foresight and imagination can prevent many problems ever arising. Tact, thoughtfulness and responsible conduct can also keep life largely problem-free.

Increased Happiness for You

Do you want to be happy? Of course, you do. And rest assured happiness is within your reach. Here's how you will achieve it.

Serve Other People

It is one of life's strange paradoxes that we find happiness for ourselves while trying to give it to others. Remember when you did someone a good turn, how smug and 'comfy' you felt inside? You were, in fact, happy. Deeply, truly happy.

The moral is obvious. If you want more happiness, help others more. Let your whole life be geared to the service of humanity. Look upon your daily work in that way. It will transform everything.

All around you people are needing help. What can you do in your spare time to relieve suffering or loneliness or poverty? How about joining some organization which exists to help others? What about social service groups, the Samaritans, or a local charity?

Or privately, are there not a few lonely old folk you could visit, or a homeless person you could befriend, or some sick people to whom you could write? In losing your life in this way, you will surely find it.

Have a Hobby

Be sure to have a hobby. Preferably let it be a creative one. You will find it thrilling to see something taking shape under your hands, whether it is a vase, a cabinet, a woollen jumper or a poem.

Money-making should not be the main object of your hobby, though if it does more than pay for itself, well and good. If your hobby makes a contribution to the well-being of others, better still. It will then make the maximum quota towards your happiness.

Learn to Like Your Job

You probably spend at least half your waking hours earning your bread and butter. To be happy, therefore, your daily work must contribute towards that state. You must get satisfactorily adjusted to your job.

First, take an interest in it. Do it to the best of your ability. Find out all you can about it. See whether you can introduce any new ideas or improvements. Discover the origins of your firm and trace its history.

Secondly, bear in mind the final results of your job. Maybe they are gleaming, useful products. Visualize people owning them and being proud of them. If you are a labourer, remember the comfort and domestic happiness your work makes possible. If you work on the land, it is a fact that people are depending on you for their food. Think of the canteens, restaurants and homes where people are eating food you helped to grow.

Thirdly, determine to excel in your work, however humble or difficult it might be. Excellence cannot long go unnoticed, and promotion will bring its own rewards, not only materially, but in a sense of satisfaction and achievement.

If the cultivation of these attitudes fails to make you like your job, think seriously about changing it.

Get Rightly Adjusted to Sex

Every normal adult has a sex instinct which is one of the strongest of natural urges. Unless you come to terms with it, it may mar the happiness you win from other sources. Be rightly adjusted to it, and it will make a major contribution to your happiness.

You live in a bi-sexual world. As a result it is stimulating, beautiful, colourful and interesting. Recognize these facts and accept your sexuality, rather than despising yourself because of it or regretting its existence.

Be sure you are enlightened on the subject. Plenty of reliable books are available. Know all the facts. Knowledge kills morbid curiosity. Cold facts, known and understood, destroy fears, misconceptions and superstitions.

Lastly, seize opportunities of mixing with the opposite sex. If you are mature, consider making a commitment to your partner. Don't let fears of insecurity lead you to postpone commitment indefinitely, nor the fact that you have not met your *ideal* partner. Paragons do not exist. Everyone has faults – yourself included.

It is a fallacy that there exists *one* person only with whom you could be happy. Given common sense and unselfishness, there are thousands with any one of whom you could be happy. Be willing, then, to take a chance.

Never consider yourself too old for love. Keep yourself clean, interesting and as attractive as possible. A charming partner could well be just round the corner, regardless of age.

Have Some Social Life

Man is a gregarious animal; he hates to be alone and he seeks the company of his fellows. To be completely happy, therefore, see you have sufficient social intercourse. Join a club, society, church or organization. This will prevent you from becoming too preoccupied with yourself. It will help to make you approachable, friendly and popular. These qualities alone will bring a quota of happiness.

When with others, seek to give rather than sit back and wait to receive. Make your contribution to the conversation; play your part in whatever activity is expected.

If you are reserved, think more about others than yourself. Go out of your way to be pleasant and helpful to others, especially to anyone who looks lonely. If conversation dries up, remember to ask a question which will encourage the other to talk.

Arrive at a Philosophy of Life

Many find that a belief in God gives them happiness. Others hold the atheist position with courage and resignation. Think through to one or other.

Remember, happiness is your birthright; don't be content until you get a large measure of it. Of course, no one is completely happy all the time. Frustrations, disappointments and sorrows are inevitable. They must be endured bravely, with no fuss and no self-pity. That way, it will not be long before you are happy once again.

Wider Mental Horizons

To increase your mental alertness, your zest for living and your general knowledge of life, you need to extend your mental horizons. You will begin to do this as you revive your child-hood curiosity, the spirit which kept asking questions. By developing the enquiring mind you will put yourself in the company of explorers, scientists and inventors; you will come to understand the world in which you live, and that is the aim of all education.

Carry out the following suggestions:

Consult Your Encyclopaedia

These treasuries of knowledge should be used far more than they are. Much time, labour and money go into their produc-tion. Get a set into your home at all costs even though it means buying it in weekly parts or by monthly instalments.

If this is out of the question, the reference room of your local library is bound to possess one. Look in and browse through it whenever you are passing or have an hour or two to spare. Better than browsing is to have several definite subjects to look up, so keep a list. Whenever a topic crosses your path which arouses your interest or about which you realize your shortcomings, jot it down, so that your time with the ency-clopaedia will be really profitable. The articles are always by reliable authorities and illustrations are plentiful and good. No field of knowledge or human activity is neglected.

Use Your Public Library

The staff at public libraries are invariably helpful and ready to place their knowledge, time and skill at the disposal of the enquirer. Often a telephone call is sufficient. A poster in one library typifies the spirit of them all: 'Whenever you want to know anything, ask the public library to help you.'

A library has unusual facilities for gaining information. Some of the staff, too, are excellent fact-finders. Remember, too, the remarkable network of co-operation which exists between libraries, making it possible for them to obtain for you – merely for the cost of return postage or less – almost any book you care to ask for. The notice board at your public library is well worth regular inspection. It will keep you acquainted with local cultural events like lectures and exhibitions, and also inform you of the activities of various societies and clubs dedicated to the widening of mental horizons.

Visit Museums

Most of us have recollections of trailing wearily around museums with a school party. Such memories tend to keep us away from them in adult years. This is unfortunate because museums have much to offer the curious adult mind, and they have changed a great deal over the years.

Make a point of revisiting the older, well-known museums, and be sure to go to any museum which comes within your orbit, for example, when on holiday.

In a museum, carefully labelled and interestingly arranged, are the fruits of years of discovery and research. Thousands of fascinating exhibits will add to your general knowledge and increase your understanding and appreciation of both your global and local environment.

Ideally, a visit should have a purpose, some particular objects to study or questions to answer. Most museums contain so much that you may be overwhelmed unless you narrow your interest. A hasty or purposeless visit may do little more than give a general idea of what is to be found there.

Many museums arrange lectures and films, or provide tours or recorded commentaries. Make use of these facilities.

Attend Public Lectures

As a member of the public, *such lectures are for you!* Be on the look out for posters advertising them – on station platforms and outside evening institutes and churches, in the literary weeklies. Various bodies are responsible for these lectures, varying from a nearby university to the local horticultural or literary society. Subjects covered range from architecture to Buddhist philosophy. Admission to most is free or a nominal charge only is made.

Most lecturers reserve time at the end to answer questions from the audience. Overcome your fears and seize these opportunities. Never be afraid to ask questions; they do not reveal ignorance so much as a lively and enquiring mind. Those who have made the greatest contribution to Man's advance have done so because they learned to pose questions. You will certainly widen your own mental horizons as you do the same.

Read Widely

The subject of reading has been considered in Step 13, but it must obviously be mentioned in this step. Here is the way, *par excellence*, of overcoming the circumscribing factors of duty, environment and lack of money. Through literature you may pass to new worlds, to heightened sensitivity, to wider understanding. Read, read, read: newspapers, magazines, above all, books – fiction and non-fiction, sacred and secular, diaries and biographies, plays, poetry, allegories, essays and novels. 'Reading maketh a full man,' wrote Francis Bacon, three centuries ago. 'Read, not to contradict and confute, nor to believe and take for granted, nor to find talk and discourse, but to weigh and consider.'

Use Television and Radio

The programmes put out on the air are a mixed bag. They have to be to cater for all tastes. They may act as stimulant or soporific; the choice is yours.

Used discriminatingly they are a wonderful way of widening mental horizons. You may use them to learn a language, follow a course of study or become familiar with the world's best music. You may visit the Antarctic, cross the Sahara or travel down the Nile. You may be a spectator at a heart operation, watch a primitive tribe go to war or have a front seat at the coronation of a sovereign. Whichever you choose, you will be widening your mental horizons.

No More Woolly Thinking

You spend the best part of your waking life thinking, so you had best check you are doing it properly. Some think in the right way, coming to valid or trustworthy conclusions. Many think loosely, unreliably, frequently arriving at false conclusions. As your personality is influenced by what you think and by the conclusions you arrive at, it is important to think validly.

Developing Your Powers of Thought

Man's progress has been painfully slow because the majority have found real thought either impossible or distasteful. As Sir Joshua Reynolds said: 'There is no expedient to which a man will not resort to avoid the real labour of thinking.'

To become a thinker you merely have to *start* thinking, really thinking. As no-one ever became proficient at public speaking until they started to speak in public, so you will never become a thinker *unless you make a start*. Perseverance will then lead to proficiency provided you avoid certain errors to be outlined.

Any reading matter will provide material to start you thinking. As you read, challenge. That is the secret of initiating thought. Never accept passively what you read. Ask: *Is this statement true, or only partially so?* How does it measure up with your experience or knowledge of history or the world?

Pause frequently and think about what you are reading. The enemies of thought are haste and impatience. Better to read *one* paragraph and allow it to evoke thought, than scamper through an entire book. When you think over a paragraph, it becomes part of your experience, and you remember it.

Another way to spark off your thinking is to challenge statements heard or read with the simple interrogatives – *How? When? Why? Who? Where? What?* Having posed these questions, try to answer them. Don't rest content until you have thought through to a satisfactory answer.

Joining a local discussion group and engaging in conversation on serious subjects are excellent ways of provoking thought. Until one has to clothe thoughts in words which will be carefully considered by others, there is a tendency not to think through to a definite opinion or to clarify ideas.

Beware False Reasoning

Processes of thinking which are untrustworthy and lead to invalid conclusions are known as *fallacies*. The more common ones are indicated in what follows.

Much reasoning takes the form of 'drawing an analogy'. The gold of New South Wales was discovered this way. A man named Hargreaves noticed that the mountains there were very similar to those in California where he had been gold-digging. He argued that if they were alike in *one* respect, they might be in another. In this case he was right, gold *was* there. But this simple type of reasoning is apt to be unreliable as the following story will show.

A professor was staying in Norway where mushrooms are seldom eaten. One day he found some and took them back to his hostess to be cooked. In an attempt to please him, Norwegian friends then presented him with gifts of *toadstools!* Because the two fungi are like in some respects, the false analogy was drawn that they are alike in *all*. Beware of this false reasoning in everyday life – things similar are not necessarily identical.

Another fallacy consists in taking for granted the very thing to be proved. This is known as *begging the question*. It occurs in various forms, some difficult to detect. Perhaps its most common guise is when we give something a name, imagining that by so doing we have explained it. For example, when a child asks why he can see through glass, his father may reply sagely: 'Because it is transparent.'

To think that a statement or doctrine is necessarily untrue because its protagonists are rogues or hypocrites is another form of invalid reasoning; it is known as *argumentum ad hominem*.

A more subtle form of erroneous thinking is to assume a position is disproved merely because its protagonists fail to prove it. The fault here lies with the protagonists and not necessarily with the position they hold.

The making of false generalizations is another example of fallacious thought. We all love to make the sweeping statement which is, in fact, based on very limited experience. The man who has spent a few hours in Colombo on his way to Australia and made several friendly contacts, may for ever afterwards airily assert that the Sinhalese are an extremely charming people.

To draw conclusions from a few instances like this is known as arguing from the particular to the general. The reverse process may also lead into error. What is true of a great many things and as a general rule, is not necessarily true of *every* case.

Argumentum ad vulgum consists of appealing to a crowd for its verdict, or the citing of numbers to support a line of argument. A favourable response from a crowd is no proof that the speaker is right, for it is comparatively easy to play upon the emotions of an audience.

It is similarly fallacious to quote as proof the support of famous or brilliant people. Those who hold differing views could do the same. In any case, even celebrities may be mistaken.

Perhaps the greatest enemy of clear, straight thinking is emotion. When we feel deeply about some issue, it is difficult to survey it impartially. Unconsciously or otherwise, we tend to distort the true picture, ignoring, suppressing, or 'forgetting' some facts, highlighting or exaggerating others.

Thinking is Free

Three centuries ago William Camden wrote: *Thoughts are free from toll.* That is still true. Thinking remains not only man's highest and noblest activity but one of the few things he may do without having to pay. A recent advertisement echoed Camden's words: *To think is not expensive. It needs no apparatus, no personnel, no premises. The only equipment is one's head; the gears and pinions of the brain, and the lever that sets them turning. Everyone can be a thinker...*

Despite that wonderful possibility and the 'inexpensiveness' of thought, comparatively few seriously indulge. It is often avoided as boring, unproductive and liable to lead into trouble. In fact, it is never the first two, though it may bring a hornets' nest about our ears, as many progressive thinkers have painfully discovered. Be that as it may, if you are determined to improve your mind, you *must* do much thinking. To do so will increase your understanding of life and the universe, and lead you to at least a measure of truth; it will enable you to live at a deeper level; it may line your pockets; it will certainly help you to play a part – however infinitesimal – in man's slow progression from brutehood.

A More Imaginative You

Avoid the error of thinking that a good imagination is the possession solely of children and people like writers and artists. In fact, imagination is part of everyone's mental equipment and can be developed to advantage. The writer Somerset Maugham, whose imagination gained him fame and fortune, wrote: 'Imagination grows by exercise, and, contrary to common belief, is more powerful in the mature than the young.'

All kinds of people in the past have been imaginative. They are the creative thinkers who have given us inventions like the pulley, pump, cog-wheel, printing press, electric light bulb, radio, jet propulsion and space capsules. With your present imagination developed you might well give some similar boon to mankind, but even if you do not, you could certainly make your own life and that of your dependants happier and more exciting.

Here are few suggestions for improving your imagination.

1. Read the first page of any children's story and then finish the story in your own way.
2. Listen to children at play.
3. Tell stories to children – remember, *anything* may happen.
4. When you read or hear of events, try to *see* them in your mind's eye.
5. Take any commonplace object and ask yourself how it could be improved.
6. Try to solve problems like reducing accidents in the home or on the roads.

7. About anything ask: *What would happen if these were made shorter? Longer? Thicker? Packed differently? Grouped with something else?* Questions of this kind will spark off your creative imagination.

Begin applying whatever imagination you now have in the spheres of:

Your Home. Must you live where you do? Could you live in a healthier or more pleasant area? The world is a big place. Use your imagination – it is the first step towards action.

How might you improve the inside of your present home? Think creatively. With a little effort, enthusiasm and cash, you can probably transform it. And how about the garden? Could you transform that? Imagine the improvements, and then act.

Your Work. Can you improve your own working conditions? How could you be more useful to your employer? How could time, labour, materials be saved? Think creatively. If you are an employer, how could you make your staff happier and more productive? Would *you* work well if you were in their place? Need old regulations still apply?

Your Relationships. Begin using your imagination in this important sphere. How can you reduce friction? Show yourself more friendly? In what ways could you make yourself a better partner, or sibling, or parent? Think and act. Imagination can change your world.

Your Achievements. Use your imagination here. Visualize yourself being what you aspire to be, doing what you want to do. It is not enough merely to make up your mind. Create success images day by day. Perhaps in the past you have always painted negative pictures. That was an unwise use of your imagination. In future, positive pictures only. Let imagination be your friend!

Your Personality. Use imagination to help you overcome undesirable habits or tendencies. If you are reserved or bad-tempered, if you stammer or blush, see yourself free from these drawbacks. Stop brooding on past failures. Paint success pictures daily. Develop a good self-image. The secret image of yourself which you have tucked away in your mind has already been determining your behaviour for years. It is this which has set limits to what you attempt and therefore to your achievement. Modify your self-image and you modify your behaviour.

Set about formulating *now* a vivid and detailed picture of the person you wish to become. Cling to this image and sooner or later you will measure up to the stature your own mind has created.

How true are John Masefield's words: '*Man's body is faulty, his mind untrustworthy, but his imagination has made him remarkable.*'

Project After Project

One of the secrets of happiness is to keep busy. To launch out upon one project after another, to be planning the next before the current one is finished – this is the path to satisfying living.

Especially is the above true when we do things we really like doing. Perhaps you say, 'I like doing nothing.' The author does too, but you will agree that you have enjoyed greatest satisfaction when you have been busily occupied with some worthwhile project. See to it, then, that the greater part of your precious leisure is devoted to doing things, making things, achieving things.

It is normal and natural to be active and creative. During the long aeons of our primitive past, we filled our days with hunting or growing food, treating skins, making weapons or canoes, constructing huts, creating pottery or ornaments, engaging in tribal dances and ceremonies, placating spirits, making love and fighting.

Many modern day needs are met with little effort. It is important therefore that we keep busy by finding worthwhile projects, activities which will make demands on the mind and body, and challenge skill and ingenuity.

Remember, being busy doesn't destroy peace of mind – it creates it! Idleness and consequent boredom are the trouble-makers. They give us time to smart under imagined grievances, chafe under emotionally-induced aches and pains, wallow in self-pity, and droop in depression and despair.

'There's no way out of it,' writes R.A. Jackson in his unusual and delightful little book *How to Like People*, 'you must have a project going, and work at it. To be a man, to have any balance at all, any fellow-feeling, to have something to think and something to say, you must be working on something.'

That is good advice. Be sure to follow it. And as you do so, you'll experience the following benefits.

Your Health Will Improve

As you pass your leisure occupied with satisfying projects, your general health will improve. That is because you will be happier due to the satisfying of one of your basic needs – to create. The intricate mechanisms of the body always function smoothly when the mind is happy. In other words, you will now be enjoying emotionally-induced health. The killers and the disease generators are the negative emotions like jealousy, resentment, hate, envy, pessimism, worry; but you have little time, energy or desire for these when you are busy with a project.

Your Mind Will Keep Alert

Your most treasured possession cannot deteriorate when it is kept busy grappling with project after project. Consider what is involved.

First, conceiving the idea, whether it's building a shed, making a swimming pool, raising money for a charity, improving your home, painting a picture, writing a book, spring-cleaning, learning a language or raising a prize chrysanthemum.

Second, the planning of the project: how long it will take, how to go about it, where to work, what materials to use, how much it will cost.

Third, the actual accomplishment of the project: wrestling with problems which arise, reading the necessary books, acquiring new skills, imposing your will on matter, and making yourself competent if not perfect.

All these make demands on mental powers and help to improve their quality.

You See Things in Truer Perspective

Doing things you like doing is therapeutic in the extreme. You face life's problems so much more sanely and surely when you have plenty of recreational activity. Boring chores, heartbreaking duties, daily tasks, never seem quite so bad when you return to them after a spell on a satisfying project. You see then that woes and afflictions and duties are only a part of life. There is spring as well as winter.

What is more, keeping busy on a project helps you to recover from life's calamities. While hands and mind are busily employed, wounds heal. Time carries out its blessed therapy, and self-pity is kept at bay. So next time life hurts you, turn to some absorbing project without delay.

You Are Easier to Live With

The joys of creativity will shed a golden aura over your whole personality. You will be less irascible, better balanced, more fun-loving, more relaxed. Achievement and genuine effort will make you feel rightly proud of yourself, and self-respect, as pointed out elsewhere, makes it easier to like others. A virtuous circle is initiated. And of course, your very achievements will also earn you respect.

Keeping busy with projects increases your zest for living; it will put a sparkle in your eye and a spring in your step. You'll always have something to talk about, something to hurry home to, something to anticipate.

Another welcome by-product is increased self-confidence. You become a smiler and a winner. You fall in love with life.

Examine your present way of living. Are you a project person? What are you working on now? What do you plan to do next? If you cannot give positive answers, get launched on some project with the minimum delay. Once you have tasted the joys of project-living, you will adopt it as a way of life and never depart from it.

Going the Extra Mile

'Hi, you! Get hold of this pack! And look sharp about it!' The tanned legionary slipped his heavy gear from powerful shoulders and hailed the passing civilian whose gaze seemed intent upon the horizon.

Such an incident must have taken place often in the subject territories of Ancient Rome. You refused to carry the pack a thousand paces on pain of severe punishment. At the end of that distance, most victims dumped it down with a curse. If they could contrive to land it on the soldier's pet corn, they did!

Jesus of Nazareth, in an attempt to introduce a better spirit into human relationships, told his disciples to shock the tough infantrymen. Their packs were to be carried *an extra mile* (Matthew's Gospel, Chapter 5, verse 41).

This spirit of the extra mile is one well worth cultivating. It is one of the secrets of happy, therefore successful living; for what life can be called successful if it is not happy?

Here's how it works in the sphere of *duty*. A harassed mother with shopping bag, toddler and push-chair is struggling to board a bus. The driver is not paid to jump on to the pavement and help her, but does so. The mother is grateful; the driver feels good. The monotony and drabness of the day has been transformed by one little act. For a moment the driver was a knight in shining armour, thoughtful, patient, tender. The extra mile ennobles all who walk it.

The teacher is not paid to give extra tuition to the slow plodder; she isn't paid to produce a play after school hours; or take a party to Spain: but she does these things. It invests her life with greater significance, improves relationships with her pupils, and makes her feel she wouldn't change her job for all the world. There is no life which cannot be immeasurably enriched by this spirit. How about giving yourself a daily injection?

The Extra Mile of Service

All duty is transformed if you regard it as service to the community. But think now of voluntary work in your leisure time.

Millions have never entertained the idea. They are entirely enslaved by self. They think only of their own comfort and enjoyment. They have never heard that 'It is a happier thing to serve than be served.'

You don't *have* to engage in this kind of service. You could refuse and still be a respectable citizen; it is, indeed, the *extra* mile. Yet thousands testify that every pace of that mile brings rich dividends. Like the quality of mercy, it is twice blessed.

Besides the gratifying knowledge that you have helped others, service widens horizons. It frees from the domination of self. Petty aches, troubles and desires are forgotten when you grapple with another's problems. Service makes you a bigger person – more understanding, more sympathetic and much happier. In other words it makes you more successful in the art of living.

The Extra Mile of Thoughtfulness

Every day thousands suffer and weep because people are thoughtless. If you would live truly successfully, you must often walk this extra mile. It will cost you time and trouble, even expense. But it will invest your personality with a golden aura and you'll stand head and shoulders above the thoughtless ones.

This thoughtfulness will take myriad forms. It may mean dropping a word of appreciation to a shop assistant who has been helpful or sending a few flowers to a lonely neighbour in hospital or dropping a Christmas card to a pensioner living in one room. It may lead you to give the window-cleaner a cup of tea or cheer the postman with a word of sympathy as he plods through the slush with your letters.

Captain Falcon Scott went the extra mile when, writing his last documents with numbed fingers as he waited for death, he penned a note to the wife of his colleague Dr Wilson, telling of her husband's heroism.

Thoughtfulness will teach you how to reprimand or correct people without hurting them; for rest assured only if you have not hurt them will you have achieved anything.

The Extra Mile of Gratitude

This old world is crying out for gratitude. Everyone likes to be thanked, to feel that what they have done is appreciated.

Are you grateful to friends for a pleasant evening or a delightful weekend? Then don't merely thank them when you leave. Go the extra mile and send them a note of thanks and perhaps a small gift.

Are you grateful to that surgeon whose skill saved you years of agony or embarrassment, your life even? Did you ever voice your thanks? Lots of people don't bother. They make a big mistake. They say either, 'She was only doing her job; she doesn't need my thanks,' or 'I suppose everyone is gushing with gratitude and she must get stacks of grateful letters. She'll guess I'm grateful and won't need me to say so!'

Remember that doctors are human and their hearts glow when they're appreciated, as yours does. They'll do their work all the better in the future if you walk the extra mile of gratitude.

Ask yourself whether you could gladden a few hearts around you by showing gratitude. Did you ever thank your old teachers, or the teachers of your children? Did you ever thank, really thank, people like the postman, the dustmen or the paper-boy? Ever dropped a note of thanks to a pilot or a ship's commander to whose skill you owe your life?

A good criterion for measuring your success in life is the number of people you have made happy. Here is a certain way of increasing that number.

The Extra Mile of Generosity

Because of innate selfishness, most of us find it easier to be mean than generous. If we can *get* rather than *give*, we feel we have scored. We love to strike a hard bargain, to *sell* something for which we have no use. We are gratified if we can sell for more than we gave. In consequence, generous deeds are so rare they provide topics for conversation.

But meanness is, in fact, short-sighted. In reality, we rob ourselves of a light heart and the satisfaction of knowing we have helped another.

'Give and it shall be given unto you, good measure, pressed down and running over.' Jesus was enunciating a fundamental law of life. The measure of our giving is the measure of our getting – in friendship, love, joy, even material blessings. The mean selfish life builds its own prison walls and passes sentence of solitary confinement.

Are you making a gift? Go the extra mile. Study the interests of the recipient, spend as much as you can afford and then add a little more!

STEP 21

Being a Better Parent

If you are not already a parent you may well be one some day. If you are already a good parent then you will want to be a better one.

No parent wants to ruin their child's future. Yet this happens all too often. It is done not by physical cruelty but by wounding a child's mind, and this is done unwittingly.

Psychology has revealed that many of the emotional troubles which bedevil adult life have their origin in the earliest years of infancy and were initiated by well-meaning but blundering parents. The moral is that parents should acquaint themselves with some of the findings of psychology on this matter. Many useful and readable books are available. Until these are read, the following paragraphs may be helpful.

A young infant doesn't think and can barely see. He is conscious only of what he can *feel*. He therefore needs the utmost security and comfort, particularly those sensual comforts deriving from proximity to the mother's breast. During the early months a baby cannot have too much affection, too many assurances of love and acceptance.

Attempts at 'potty training' should never be enforced by signs of anger or withdrawal of love.

When a baby begins to play with his sexual organs, allow him to do so. No harm comes of this, but damage may be done by smacks and signs of disapproval.

Always bear in mind that a child is a person. The fact that a child is small makes no difference. Soon your child will have a temperament, feelings, hopes, fears, loves, hatreds, just as

78

adults, and will be just as sensitive as adults – probably more so. Children like to be praised and feel successful as adults do. They value possessions and like their comforts too. Like adults, too, a child wants to feel secure, loved, wanted.

Adults hate to be frustrated; so does a child. Adults call angry reactions a tantrum; there is no one to call *their* reactions anything! As a person and not a paragon, your child will sometimes be lazy, thoughtless, ungrateful, untidy.

Bearing these things in mind, always be considerate with a child. Never expect too much. Your child is an ordinary, erring human – small and weak.

A child has not yet fully learned to co-ordinate movements, and at times will be clumsy and will make mistakes. But children have plenty of native confidence. Foster this; don't squash it by discouragement and sarcasm. Co-ordination will come as you provide opportunities to practise and experiment, and as you are lavish with encouragement.

See that you are never an aggressive, unpredictable tyrant. Instead, aim at being a reliable friend. Suggest and advise rather than command and bully. If you *must* impose your will, give reasons rather than be arbitrary.

The Importance of Play

You must appreciate the importance of play in a child's life; it widens the child's experience, creates things, develops the imagination and gains various compensations. Through play, a child prepares for the world of reality awaiting.

Encourage your child to play by providing materials like sand, water, empty boxes, cartons, a few small planks, a hammer and nails, a dozen or so bricks. A good ruse is to dig a hole in the garden two or three feet deep, banking up the earth around the edges. A toddler will be amused for hours sliding in and climbing out, at the same time learning to take risks and overcome difficulties. Remember, a busy child is a happy child and no trouble. Such a child is most likely to grow into a happy, well-balanced adult.

Encouragement and Example

When difficulties arise, don't rush to your child's aid. See if your child can overcome them unaided. This will develop self-reliance. When your child is really beaten you can suggest solutions or give a helping hand. You don't want your child to grow up always looking to you for help.

When you have children, you can't expect to have a spotless, tidy home or an immaculate garden. You must take your choice – home and garden or a happy, self-confident child. No visitor will think worse of you because it is evident a child is about the place.

A good rule with children is 'Don't say *Don't* if *Do* will do.' In other words give positive guidance rather than negative commands. A psychologist was spending a weekend with a family. Feeling the number of commands given to the child there was high, she decided to count them. In two hours the little boy was given 120 commands, 73 of them negative in content. This is deplorable and must be avoided.

Bear in mind that a child learns largely by imitation. A child will learn to speak that way, which amounts to learning a language. If you do not wish your child to learn bad habits, bad manners or poor speech, you must never be guilty of them yourself. If you want your child to be truthful, never tell lies – as your child may find out! Imitation is one of the greatest educative factors in childhood. Exploit it for good.

You are largely what your parents made you. Your

children will be largely what you make them. Here lies the responsibility of parenthood.

Some Important Factors

Never deceive your child, especially about birth and sexual matters. When asked, tell your child without embarrassment that they grew snugly inside mummy until they were old enough to come out. Generally that will be sufficient and the matter will be shelved until puberty. On no account keep up the stork or gooseberry-bush yarns.

Well before adolescence a boy should know of the onset of nocturnal emissions and a girl of the monthly period. They should also know the main facts of conception and the process of birth. If you cannot bring yourself to talk of these things, see that suitable literature is available.

It is most important that a child should be aware of constant, harmonious relationships between parents. If you *must* quarrel with your partner, don't do it before your child; and make up before a rift can be sensed. When parents quarrel, a child feels insecure and loyalties are divided. For the same reasons it is unwise to speak disparagingly of your partner before your child or be disloyal in any way. Failings should be glossed over, never enlarged.

You will doubtless be anxious that your child should develop a sound character. Never resort to nagging which cannot build character. A good character is the voluntary adoption of good habits. That adoption will take place only if the habits are associated with pleasant consequences. You cannot therefore be too generous with rewards and praise.

Bringing up children to become happy, self-reliant, well-integrated personalities is an art, one which is mastered only by much thought, imagination and self- discipline.

STEP 22

All Serene

Serene folk enjoy life rather than endure it. Their presence helps and inspires others. Instead of being victims of circumstances, they possess a happy knack of being masters of any situation. The serene types are always healthier than others and generally live longer. Like to join the serene set? Here's how you qualify for membership.

Reach A Balanced Evaluation of Yourself

Many people get tense because they take life and themselves too seriously. They see themselves out of proportion; self looms so large that they begin to regard themselves as indispensable.

To become a serene person you need to realize that you are only one of millions and that you are not irreplaceable. Accept this, even be glad about it. Further, realize that compared with the vast, awesome powers of nature, you are insignificant. Thinking of the immensity of space, the vastness of the oceans, the might of the winds, you become conscious that you are but a speck, a straw, a leaf.

But do not allow this to depress you. After all, it is the lot of humanity, even the greatest. If you are insignificant, you are insignificant among equals. You may feel humble, but there is no need to feel inferior. Accept that you have talents, slight though they may be, and that you have a unique contribution to make to life.

Thus by facing facts, you will reach a balanced evaluation of yourself, and the foundation for serenity is laid.

Know Your Own Character

Many people do not understand their own natures and in consequence they suffer distress and conflict. They are puzzled by the seething desires and emotions they find bubbling up within themselves. But there is no cause for alarm. Here, as in every sphere, knowledge banishes fear and superstition.

Thanks to the researches of psychologists, Man is in a better position to understand himself than ever before in his long history. It seems that the typical person has certain basic urges which may be listed as follows:

1. To have food and bodily comfort – to feel secure.
2. To wield power in some form – to control others – to feel significant or important.
3. To create – to construct.
4. To protect the weak and helpless.
5. To find out – to understand – to be curious.
6. To escape from danger – to preserve oneself.
7. To gain, possess, acquire.
8. To laugh.
9. To fight – to repel the unpleasant.
10. To submit to a stronger force – to appeal for help.
11. To mix with others – to be one of a group – to be like others of one's own set.
12. To mate with a member of the opposite sex – to reproduce.

According to Freud, the last of these, the sexual instinct, is the strongest, and there is plenty of evidence to support the view.

People with strong religious views or who come from strictly religious families sometimes have difficulty in accepting their sexuality as a normal constituent of their personalities. They fail to realize that the sexual instinct is not, of itself, sinful. In consequence they suffer untold torments, regarding every sex impulse and thought as a 'temptation', something to be resisted and overcome. If you are in this category, you need to rethink the issue.

It is useful to become acquainted with the above list as it will help you to understand not only your own behaviour but that of others. With understanding comes tolerance and charity, and you take a big step towards the serene temperament.

A Knowledge of History Helps

Some knowledge of the past will help you to face the present and future with equanimity, to see things in correct perspective. You need to appreciate something of the staggering story of the earth's crust as revealed by geology. You ought to have some idea of the fantastic evolutionary development of plant and animal life. You must be aware that man has been wandering about in primitive hunting groups many times longer than the comparatively short time he has been civilized.

You should be familiar with the main events of these last millenia – the rise and fall of empires, the principal figures, the master minds, the unprecedented acceleration of progress and knowledge this century.

Such knowledge will help you to remain unperturbed when alarmists tell you that Man will soon annihilate himself or that the end of the world is near. It will also increase your fortitude in bearing your own misfortunes.

Above all, to realize that you are playing a part, however infinitesimal, in some gigantic scheme, foreseen or otherwise, will enable you to regard your life as having purpose and significance.

Learn to Relax

Make relaxation a habit. At odd moments during the day when opportunity occurs, flop down in a chair or on a bed or sofa. Relax every muscle. Close your eyes. Pass your fingertips lightly over your forehead several times and let your face melt into a smile. Do this also when you go to bed. You'll enjoy better sleep.

While working, conserve your energies. By forethought reduce unnecessary jaunts upstairs (unless, of course, you feel you need the exercise!). Avoid standing if you can work equally well sitting down. Place tools and materials handy so as to reduce movement as much as possible. Such practices reduce strain and fatigue.

Do get into the habit of smiling readily. You cannot be tense when you are smiling, and you look so much more attractive! You'll know more serenity of mind when you smile more.

The benefits of having a hobby have been extolled earlier, in Step 19. There's nothing like it for helping you to relax and to develop a serene temperament.

Eradicate Hatred and Worry

It is surprising how many charming people allow hatred to fester in their minds for years. The author recently chatted with two elderly gentlemen who appeared the embodiment of geniality and harmlessness. Yet each declared his intense hatred for another most vehemently. In both instances the person hated had been guilty of a trivial misdemeanour years before. See you don't fall into this trap. And with hatred banish jealousy, envy and bitterness.

It is worth stressing that worry is productive of nothing but furrowed brows, nervous breakdowns and gastric ulcers. It solves no problems (see Step 14). You'll know little serenity if you allow yourself to become a worrier.

Enrich Your Life Now

Do you sometimes feel your life is drab, unsatisfactory, superficial? There's no reason for it to continue that way. You may enrich it in many ways, for example:

Tune in to the Beautiful

It is a well-known fact that we notice what interests us. Why not use this fact to canalize more and more beauty into your life? Become interested in the beautiful. Begin looking for it and you will find it all around you.

Nature provides an unending pageant of beauty. Start by looking at the clouds, *really looking at them*. Whether white, wispy and ethereal or massively grey and awe-inspiring, they are worthy of frequent observation.

Ever seen apple-blossom in sunlight, backed by a clear blue sky? That takes some beating. So does a cedar outlined against a sunset. How about sweet peas for fragrance and delicacy of form and colour? Ever noticed the sheen on well-groomed hair? And what of the uninhibited laughter of a toddler?

Learning to appreciate music is another means of channelling infinite beauty into your life. A violin concerto by Mozart or Beethoven, a nocturne of Chopin or a symphony of Schubert or Haydn, all contain passages of rare and unforgettable loveliness and delicacy. Be sure that prejudice does not keep you from this fountain of truly satisfying sound.

The great paintings of the world are another source of beauty to be tapped. What wealth of colour is there, what grace and elegance, what love of living, what beauty of line and composition! There is no life which cannot be immeasurably enriched by studying the art treasures of the world. They will make you more observant, more beauty conscious, more aware of the vagaries of light, the nobility of carriage and movement, the elegance of dress, the poignancy of suffering and grief. As we saw in Step 13, the reading of good novels and poetry can have equally quickening effects. For enriching your life be sure to tune in to beauty.

Enjoy the Necessary

So much precious time is devoted to necessary activities, why not determine that they are going to enrich your life?

You *have* to eat and drink. Why not really enjoy doing so? Savour your food and drink to the full. Let them give you pleasure. You may become an epicure without degenerating into a gourmand.

You *have* to commute daily? Why not use the time – often two or three hours a day – to enrich your life? Spend some of it observing the people around you. How about trying to get into conversation with at least one fellow-commuter each day? But spend the bulk of your travelling-time reading good novels or educational books. This way you should be able to get through thirty or forty books a year, perhaps more.

Alternatively, why not study a language on your outward journey while you are fresh, and a novel on the way home?

You *have* to sleep. Don't resent it – enjoy it! Invest in a really comfortable bed and pillow. Have light, warm blankets, and coloured sheets. Make your bedroom a beautiful place, and look forward to your sleeping time when you may relax in comfort and safety. You spend a third of your life in bed. Let the experience enrich your life. About a fifth of your sleep-time is spent in the strange world of dreams. Find out all you can about this phenomenon; it's a fascinating study leading to greater self-knowledge. Interest in dreams adds a further dimension to the nightly session of unconsciousness.

You probably *have* to work for your living. For the greater part of every day you cannot pursue your own interests, and if you're like most people you resent this arrangement. But is this wise? Why not begin looking forward to this great consumer of your limited time? Don't work to live – live to work. Change your attitude completely. Regard your job as an opportunity for service, for achievement, for self-development. Accept your daily tasks as challenges and resolve to win. Do the best you can every day. That way satisfaction lies, contentment at the day's end. That way the humblest job is worthy to be called a profession, a vocation.

Show ingenuity and enterprise in your work. Work with a will. It can be fun if you go about it the right way and in the right spirit. Ask yourself: *How can I improve my performance, increase my output, raise the quality? Is it possible to tackle old jobs in a new way? Am I keeping abreast of the latest methods and ideas?*

One important factor in enjoying your work is to get on well with the people around you. Why not embark on a policy of improved relations? Show yourself friendly and good-humoured. Go out of your way to help others. You will soon find things improving. Remember the strange but valid paradox, mentioned elsewhere in these pages but worth reiteration, *before you can like others you must first like yourself*, i.e., come to accept yourself as a worthwhile person of integrity. From self-respect will come respect for others. They, sensing your respect, will give you theirs and the basis of good relationships is laid.

Say 'No' to the Negative

Are you living in a sea of negation, always saying 'No' to life –
declining invitations, rejecting opportunities, saying you can't
do this or that, decrying yourself, despising yourself, drowning
yourself in despair and self-pity?

Perhaps you are not in that category, but consider whether
you could not enrich your life by saying 'No' less often. In fact,
why not go the whole way and resolve to make it a life-long rule
always to say 'No' to the negative! In future you go forwards not
backwards. Accept, venture, try, hope, expect, love. Forget the
depressing and rejoice in the good, the colourful, the beautiful.
Sunbathe all the year round! Life will get better and better as you
enthrone the positive. You'll enjoy sound health, you'll have
abundant vitality, you'll have love and more to spare. And of
course, all kinds of opportunities come to the positive person.

Develop your Potential

Always bear in mind that you have more ability than meets the
eye. You are, in fact, extremely versatile. As you continue saying
'No' to the negative, you will begin to see your hidden powers
developing.

'*I can*' is a wonderful key unlocking countless doors. '*I'll
try*' prises open the rustiest and most formidable locks. '*I
believe*' opens magic casements and reveals hidden treasures.

You are more skilful, more gifted, possibly more intelli-
gent than you have ever imagined. It is well within your powers
to be determined, patient, self-reliant, industrious, painstaking,
accurate, punctual, strong, helpful, responsible. You are able to
develop a better memory, a stronger will, more self-confidence,
a greater facility with words, greater organizing ability. You
can get things done.

'*It is all too obvious that, in the great majority of human beings, the greater part of their possibilities, whether physical or spiritual, intellectual or aesthetic, remains unrealised.*' That is the opinion of one of our leading biologists, Sir Julian Huxley. It is an encouraging and challenging statement. In the light of it you may go on enriching your life by calling upon your dormant powers. You may safely believe they exist and go on to exploit them to the full.

Naturally, saying 'Yes' to life will lead you to do this to a gratifying extent. Enrol for courses. Take up new hobbies. Accept greater responsibilities. Undertake untried tasks. Under the stimulus of greater demands and new challenges, your potential powers will surface. You will be surprised, and your friends will be surprised as they see the new hidden YOU emerging.

But it was only what was to be expected!